Kids Around the World Create!

Kids Around the World Create!

The Best Crafts and Activities from Many Lands

Arlette N. Braman

illustrated by Jo-Ellen Bosson

John Wiley & Sons, Inc.

New York ■ Chichester ■ Weinheim ■ Brisbane ■ Singapore ■ Toronto

This book is printed on acid-free paper. ∞

Published by John Wiley & Sons, Inc.
Published simultaneously in Canada

Design and production by Navta Associates, Inc.

The publisher and the author have made every reasonable effort to ensure that the experiments and activities in this book are safe when conducted as instructed but assume no responsibility for any damage caused or sustained while performing the experiments or activities in the book. Parents, guardians, and/or teachers should supervise young readers who undertake the experiments and activities in this book.

Library of Congress Cataloging-in-Publication Data
Braman, Arlette N.
      Kids around the world create! : the best crafts and activities
   from many lands / Arlette N. Braman.
         p.   cm.
      ISBN 0-471-29005-X (paper)
      1. Activity programs in education.   2. Handicraft—Study and
   teaching.   3. Multicultural education—Activity programs.   I. Title.
   LB1027.25.B73   1999
   372.5'5—dc21   99-12225

Printed in the United States of America
10   9   8   7   6   5   4   3   2

For Dr. Patricia Pinciotti of East Stroudsburg
University, my mentor and friend,
who helped me see this book with a new vision

Contents

Acknowledgments

I would like to say a big thanks to Callan and Abigail Braman, Gary and Greg Lewis, Elizabeth and Jill Decker, Timmy Warner, the students from Mrs. Saeger's and Mrs. Iglio's third-grade class at Hamilton Elementary School, and the students from Mrs. Wenck's fifth-grade class at the Stroudsburg Middle School for testing all of the activities in the book.

A very special thanks to my parents, Michael, Josephine, and Avis, who filled my childhood with wonderful, cultural traditions that I will always treasure.

Thank you, Philip Lee of Lee & Low Books, for giving me the most valuable critique I've ever had.

All of the following people deserve a special thanks for lending me books, offering great ideas, helping me out in a pinch, and sharing information about their cultural backgrounds: Dr. Ian H. Ackroyd-Kelly, Alfredo Bazán, Florence Bottin, Max Donkor, Dr. Sue Harlan, Maria Horn, Norman Hurst, Mary Karch, Michelle Lagos, Liz Lewis, Caroline MacPhee, Raven Manocchio, Cecil Mark, Carolyn McIntyre, Avis Neary, Boonchad Pruettipun, Nalini Rao, Liz Ruckel, Bobbie Rudnick, Lindsay Rudnick, Robin Scott, Kazu Seto, Heide and Emil Signes, Pat Soulia, Bharath Sundararaman, Johanna Weaver, and Michael Roudette, senior librarian at the Schomburg Center for Research in Black Culture.

A special thanks to the following people for allowing Gary Braman to photograph their cultural treasures: Michelle Decker for her patchwork quilt; Kathy Schenkel and Lew Taylor for the Navajo rug from their shop, Tumbleweed, in West Dennis, Massachusetts; Sarita Walcott for her Kwanzaa *kinara;* and Rampa Starr for sending the beautiful pictures of the *krathongs.*

Thanks to my best writing friends, Sue Grillo and Gwen Holmes, who unselfishly give their support, advice, and encouragement, and to my editor, Kate Bradford, for making this a pleasant and enjoyable experience.

Thanks to my children, Callan and Abigail, who always think my ideas are great, and to my husband, Gary, for his help, support, and suggestions, and for working day and night to shoot and develop photos for the book.

A Message to Kids of All Cultures

I've always enjoyed learning about different cultures and grew up in a very multicultural home (French, Polish, and Spanish). My parents filled my childhood with wonderful foods, customs, and traditions from these and other cultures, and I try to do the same with my children. Now that I'm an adult, I love to travel to different countries, meet people, share their customs, sample their foods, and learn about their world. In many ways, we are alike and enjoy the same things. But it's our differences that I find so fascinating. We all have something special to offer each other. My hope is that children everywhere, just like you, will welcome and accept the diversity that makes our world so wonderful.

All of the activities in this book will give you an opportunity to experience some of this diversity. The activities are easy to do and you should be able to find most of the supplies around your house. And remember, always clean up when you're finished. Have fun on your trip as you visit many lands.

Craft Recipes, Shopping Tips, and Helpful Hints

CRAFT RECIPES

Homemade Dough

Some of the projects in this book are made from dough. Here is an easy recipe for homemade dough you can use for most of these projects.

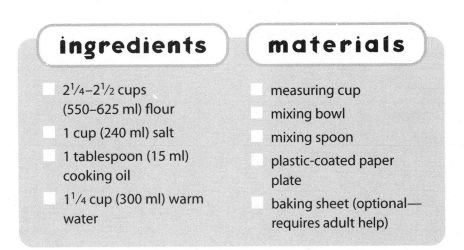

ingredients

- 2¼–2½ cups (550–625 ml) flour
- 1 cup (240 ml) salt
- 1 tablespoon (15 ml) cooking oil
- 1¼ cup (300 ml) warm water

materials

- measuring cup
- mixing bowl
- mixing spoon
- plastic-coated paper plate
- baking sheet (optional—requires adult help)

1 Mix 2¼ cups (550 ml) of flour and the salt together in the bowl. Add the oil and stir. Slowly add the water and stir. Mix with the spoon until well blended. Knead or squeeze the dough with your hands until it is smooth and firm, about 10 minutes. If the dough is too sticky, add the last ¼ cup (about 60 ml) of flour. If it's too dry, add a little more water.

2 Keep the dough in a plastic zipper bag so it won't dry out. It will last about 1 week in the refrigerator. To shape the dough, follow the directions given in the activities.

3 To air-dry your project, place it on a plastic-coated paper plate and let dry for about 5 days until very hard. Turn your project over each day so that all sides dry.

To bake your project: Place your project on a baking sheet and bake at 250°F (121°C) for about 2 to 3 hours. Always ask an adult for help when using an oven. Always use oven mitts. Check your project after *each* hour of baking. Make sure holes (like the ones in the beads you'll be making) stay opened. The holes can be reopened with the blunt end of the paintbrush. *Ask an adult for help!* Let the project cool completely.

If you don't want to make your own dough, you can buy clay that air-dries and hardens or clay that hardens in water. Most brands for kids are easy to use. Just follow the directions.

SHOPPING TIPS

You can find most of the supplies needed for these projects in your home. If you have to buy something, look in craft or art supply stores, office supply stores, large toy stores, or discount chain stores.

HELPFUL HINTS

1 Use freezer paper when you work with the homemade dough or clay. Tape a big piece of freezer paper, wax side up, to your work surface. The dough or clay won't stick to the the waxy paper.

2 If you don't have freezer paper, use a plastic tray or a plastic-coated paper plate when working with dough or clay.

3 You will need a craft paintbrush for many of the projects. Don't use ones that have thick bristles. Use craft artist brushes made for kids.

4 After your painted project dries, use a clear acrylic sealer to help protect it. Any type of clear craft sealer will work. Spray cans are easier to use. *Always use spray sealer outside with the help of an adult!*

PART ONE

Eye Dazzlers

Designs are everywhere. They dazzle the eye with color and shape. Designs can create interesting patterns like the kind found on your striped T-shirt, or they can be symmetrical like a snowflake or abstract like clouds.

All cultures create designs in the houses they build, the clothes they sew, the baskets they weave, the clay they sculpt, and the jewelry they make. A traditional house from Torajaland, in the republic of Indonesia, uses a boat-shaped design for the roof. The traditional dress of Jordanian women incorporates lines of color at the bottom and along the sides of the dress. While all cultures make similar items, each bears the distinctive design representative of the culture. A Puerto Rican seed necklace and a Sioux bear claw necklace are both jewelry. But each has a unique design.

The activities in this section will dazzle your eyes with designs from different cultures. Look all around you. You're sure to see a design somewhere.

Welcome to My Room
INDIAN WELCOME MESSAGE

Many cultures use **symmetry** (balance in which one side of a design is the mirror image of the other side) in the designs they create on their clothing, pottery, weaving, and jewelry. The English who first settled in America couldn't buy wallpaper, so they decorated the walls of their homes with stenciled designs, many of which were symmetrical. A popular design, the pineapple, meant "welcome." Early Canadian settlers made symmetrical cut-paper leaf designs as decorations to remind themselves of the coming spring.

In southern India, mothers and daughters begin their day with an interesting custom. At sunrise, they go outside and clean the porch or front steps of their home with water. After it dries, they draw a symmetrical design, called *rangoli* (pronounced ron-GO-lee), with white powder. First they make dots, then they connect the dots with lines. This design welcomes people into their home.

Each morning the women make a new symmetrical design. Some use chalk so they don't have to change the design every day. On special occasions the inside spaces of the design are filled with colors. Then the mother or daughter writes a welcome message under the design.

Look at the symmetrical Indian welcome design shown here. You can make an Indian welcome design for your bedroom door. When it's taped to your bedroom door it means "come in." If you take it off, it means "stay out."

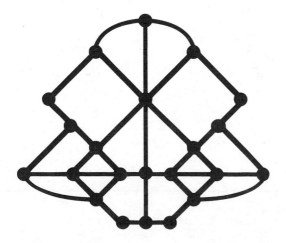

Here's What You Need

- [ ] pencil
- [ ] scrap paper
- [ ] colored construction paper
- [ ] white chalk
- [ ] colored chalk (optional)
- [ ] masking tape

Here's What You Do

1 Using pencil and scrap paper, practice a few designs of your own, or copy the design shown at the beginning of this activity. Make dots in a symmetrical pattern first. This means you make a dot on the left side of the paper, then make a dot in the same place on the right side of the paper. Connect the dots with lines.

2 Make your design on the construction paper with chalk. Remember to start with the dots. If you make a mistake, just use the back of the paper. Blow off any excess chalk dust.

art choice

For special occasions you can fill in the spaces of your design with colored chalk. Remember to keep the colors symmetrical, so that what you do on one side is done in the same place on the other side. You can also write a message under your design.

3 Tape your finished design to your bedroom door with a small piece of masking tape. *Check with an adult before you do this.* You can change your design every week.

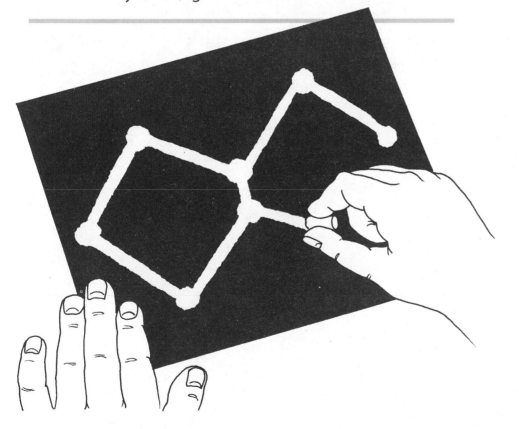

© 1999 Gary Braman

Wycinanki

In Poland, people hang symmetrical cut-paper designs called *wycinanki* (pronounced vih-chee-NON-key) inside their homes before Easter. Because farmers' wives started this tradition in the early 1800s, many of the designs are of animals, trees, or flowers. The designs remain on the walls until the following year, when they are replaced by new *wycinanki*.

The Quilting Bee
AMISH QUILT

A quilt is a blanket that is made by sewing together a top and bottom layer of cloth and stuffing the inside with a different material. To keep warm during the Middle Ages, the Crusaders lined their armor with quilting. In the fourteenth century, Europeans made quilts as bedcovers. American pioneer women are believed to be the first to have made quilts from scraps of cloth and worn-out pieces of clothing. These quilted bedcovers became known as patchwork quilts. After a while, the women wanted more design in their quilts, so they pieced together fabric to make geometric patterns, flower designs, and repeating patterns.

The **Amish** (a religious group who came to America in the 1700s from Germany and France) are famous for their beautiful patchwork quilts. The Amish of Lancaster County, Pennsylvania, are known for their quilts of solid colors and geometric designs. Many Amish still make quilts by hand and continue to shun modern conveniences such as electricity, cars, computers, and television.

Shown here are some traditional Amish quilt designs.

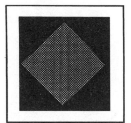

Center Diamond

Bars

Nine Patch

You won't make a whole quilt in this activity, but one block or square in an Amish quilt design called the Center Diamond. When you're finished, you can hang the quilt square in your room.

Here's What You Need

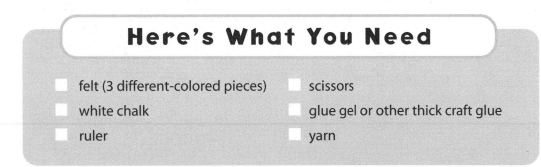

- [ ] felt (3 different-colored pieces)
- [ ] white chalk
- [ ] ruler
- [ ] scissors
- [ ] glue gel or other thick craft glue
- [ ] yarn

art choice You can pick your favorite colors for the felt pieces or choose colors the Amish use, like dark blue, green, purple, red, black, and brown.

Here's What You Do

1 You need three felt squares for your design. Each should be a different color. Use chalk to mark each measurement. Make the first square 6 by 6 inches (15 by 15 cm), the second square $4\frac{1}{4}$ by $4\frac{1}{4}$ inches (11 by 11 cm), and the third square 3 by 3 inches (7.5 by 7.5 cm). Cut out the squares.

2 Lay the largest felt square on a table or other flat surface. This square is the background of the design. Glue the medium felt square to the center of the background piece.

3 Turn the smallest felt square so that it looks like a diamond and glue it to the medium square. Let your Center Diamond design dry completely.

4 Cut three small rectangles from scraps of felt, each measuring $1\frac{1}{2}$ by 1 inch (4 by 2.5 cm). Set these aside.

5 Make a hanger by cutting a 24-inch (61-cm) strand of yarn. Lay the yarn across the *back* top edge of the Center Diamond design, spacing the yarn about $\frac{3}{4}$ inch (2 cm) down from the top edge. Glue the three small rectangles, spaced evenly apart, over the yarn. Let the glue dry completely.

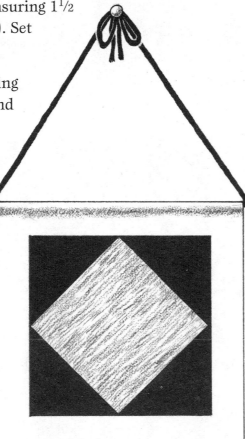

6 Tie the ends of the yarn together in a bow or knot. Hang the Center Diamond design wherever you like.

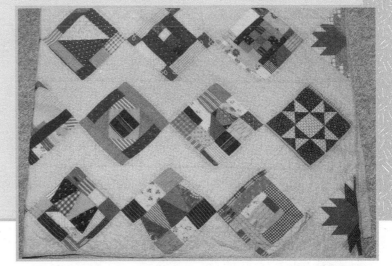

Wonderful Weaving
GUATEMALAN WEAVING

Weaving is an ancient art. Historians have found proof of weaving in all civilizations. People from the Stone Age wove with natural fibers like palm leaves to make mats. The Chinese wove with silk in 2600 B.C. Today cultures all over the world continue this art form. Colorful cloth from Ghana, a nation of western Africa, is woven in designs that look like basket weaving. This cloth is called **kente** (from the word *kenten* meaning "basket"). There are over 300 different kente patterns. Woolen **kilts** (knee-length plaid skirts with deep pleats), worn by men from the Scottish Highlands, are woven with traditional plaid designs.

Guatemalan weaving is famous for its beautiful bright colors and original eye-catching designs. (Guatemala is a country in Central America.) The Quiché, an Indian group of western Guatemala, weave colorful patterns passed down from their Mayan ancestors. Women spin the wool, dye it bright colors, and weave the thread on a backstrap loom. From this woven cloth they make blouses, shirts, blankets, hammocks, shawls, and bags. No two villages use the same designs. A native Indian can tell a person's home village by looking at the patterns on the cloth.

You can create your own Guatemalan design when you weave a bookmark using a cardboard loom.

Here's What You Need

- pencil
- ruler
- cardboard
- scissors
- yarn in bright colors like red, yellow, green, purple, black, blue, and pink

Here's What You Do

1 Draw a 3-by-7-inch (9-by-17.5-cm) rectangle on the cardboard. Cut this out. This is your cardboard loom.

2 On both short edges, cut five slits about ¹/₂ inch (1.5 cm) apart. Make each slit about ¹/₂ inch (1.5 cm) deep.

3 Cut one strand of yarn about 61 inches (155 cm) long and put it through the *bottom left* slit of the loom, leaving a 4-inch (10-cm) tail on the back of the loom. Wrap the yarn around the loom, working from bottom to top through each slit in turn. When you reach the *top right* slit, put the yarn through that slit, and leave a 4-inch (10-cm) tail on the back of the loom as shown. These vertical strands are called the *warp* strands.

4 Cut one strand of yarn to begin weaving. For narrow rows of color, strands should be between 14 and 16 inches (36 and 41 cm) long. For wider rows of color, strands should be between 18 and 22 inches (46 and 56 cm) long.

5 Start to weave at the *bottom right* of the loom. Put the strand through the bottom right slit, leaving a 4-inch (10-cm) tail on the back. To begin, follow these steps:

- **First row:** Put the strand *under* the first warp strand on the right and *over* the next. Keep weaving under and over until you reach the end of the row.

- **Second row:** Weave *over* the first warp strand on the left and *under* the next until you reach the end of that row. Continue weaving the other rows in this manner.

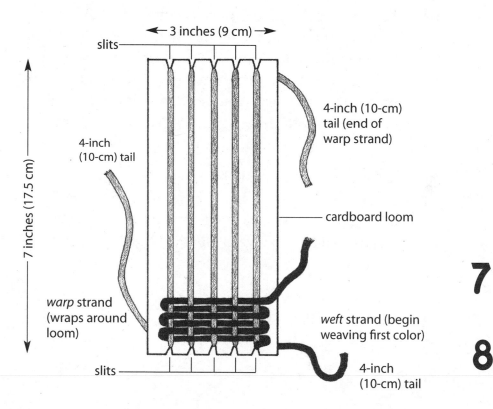

← 3 inches (9 cm) →

slits

4-inch
(10-cm) tail

4-inch (10-cm)
tail (end of
warp strand)

7 inches (17.5 cm)

cardboard loom

warp strand
(wraps around
loom)

weft strand (begin
weaving first color)

slits

4-inch
(10-cm) tail

These horizontal strands are called the *weft* strands. You want to make a tight weave, so push down or pack every row close to the one before it with your fingers.

6 Continue weaving, using different colors to create a Guatemalan design. Whenever you start a new color, weave the first row of the color the *same* way you wove the row you just finished (either under then over or over then under). Always finish the last row of the old color on the left and start the first row of the new color on the right as shown. There will be a lot of little yarn ends sticking out wherever you start or end a new color. Don't cut these until after your bookmark is finished.

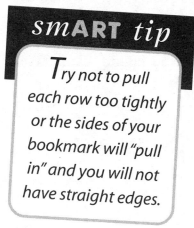

7 Continue weaving until you reach the top of the loom. Pack the rows one last time before you finish to make sure they are very close together.

8 Put the end of the strand through the top right slit, leaving a 4-inch (10-cm) tail on the back.

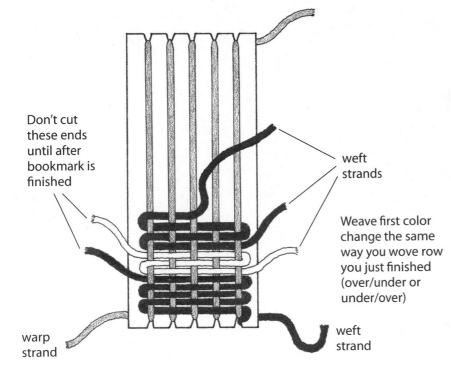

Don't cut these ends until after bookmark is finished

warp strand

weft strands

Weave first color change the same way you wove row you just finished (over/under or under/over)

weft strand

10 To make a fringe, cut the knotted warp strands to about 2 inches (5 cm). Unwind each strand.

11 Cut the little yarn ends that are sticking out of the rows by gently pulling up each yarn end and cutting it as close to the bookmark as possible without cutting any of the woven strands. Put your bookmark under a heavy book overnight to flatten it.

9 Turn the loom facedown and cut the warp strands across the middle, then turn the loom faceup again. Remove the warp strands from the slits. There will be six strands hanging from each short edge, five warp strands and one weft strand. Tie the two left strands together in a knot. Do the same for the next two strands and the last two strands. Repeat for the warp strands at the top of the bookmark.

Navajo Weaving

Another group of people known for their beautiful weaving are the Navajo Indians of North America. They create geometric patterns in their rugs and blankets. Some of the designs are complicated patterns of zigzags, crosses, and diamonds.

© 1999 Gary Braman

Saying Good-Bye
GHANAIAN ADINKRA CLOTH

S aying good-bye to a favorite teacher, a best friend who is moving, or a grandparent who has died is difficult. Many people in America wear black at funerals as a sign of grief. But black is not the universal color used for farewell. People from the South Pacific islands wear a combination of white and black to show their joy or sorrow.

In Ghana, a country in western Africa, people have an interesting way to say good-bye. At a funeral or a farewell gathering they wear clothes made from *adinkra* cloth.

(**Adinkra** is the name of a dye and it also means "good-bye" in Akana, a Ghanaian language.) This dye is used to cover the cloth with symbols that create interesting designs. Each symbol has a meaning. Sometimes a few symbols are put together to make a special message.

The *Gyaman* (pronounced JAH-mahn), a group of people from Ghana, first made these traditional symbols. When the *Asante* (pronounced ah-SAHN-tee), the largest group of people living in Ghana, conquered the Gyaman, they started using the symbols and developed new ones. To make each symbol, *adinkra* is brushed onto a stamp made from carved gourds. Then the stamp is pressed onto a section of the cloth. Bamboo combs and sticks dipped in the dye are used to make the lines around each section of cloth. This is done over and over until the symbols are transformed into beautiful patterned designs. When the cloth pieces are dry, they are sewn together with brightly colored thread.

You can make your own *adinkra* symbols on a good-bye card to give to someone you care about.

In Ghana, a russet (reddish brown) color means sadness, and this color of cloth is worn for a close relative. Other colors, like blue, may be used for other people. If you want to go with tradition, use one of these two colors for your card.

Here's What You Need

- newspapers
- piece of scrap paper, 8½ by 11 inches (21.5 by 28 cm)
- craft paintbrush
- acrylic or poster paint (black and several other, bright colors)
- variety of objects to use as stamps (small bottle cap, the head of a screw, string wrapped around a cardboard tube, dried pasta, button, or anything you like)
- pencil
- ruler
- piece of colored construction paper
- scissors
- skinny stick with a pointed tip
- small bowl of water
- paper towels
- glue (optional)
- photo (optional)

Here's What You Do

1 Spread the newspapers over your work area (a table or the floor).

2 Practice making symbols on the scrap paper first. To make symbols, brush black paint on the part of the object with the most interesting design. Press this part onto the scrap paper. Practice this step with all the objects you've selected. You'll need to brush the object with paint each time you stamp on a symbol.

3 Use the pencil to draw a 6-by-9-inch (15-by-23-cm) rectangle on the construction paper. Cut this out. Fold the paper in half to make a 4½-by-6-inch (11.5-by-15-cm) card. Open the card and lay it flat on the work area, with the outside front and back parts of the card faceup.

4 Paint several skinny lines with the pointed end of the stick to frame the front and back sections of the card. You'll need to dip the stick into the paint often. Let the lines dry completely.

5 Using your objects, stamp symbols on the front and back sections of the card, inside the painted lines. You can arrange your symbols in a patterned design. Let the stamped symbols dry completely.

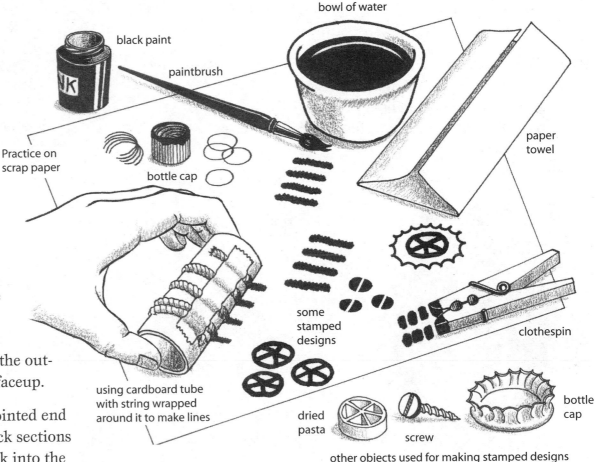

bowl of water

black paint

paintbrush

paper towel

Practice on scrap paper

bottle cap

some stamped designs

clothespin

using cardboard tube with string wrapped around it to make lines

dried pasta

screw

bottle cap

other objects used for making stamped designs

6 To make the brightly colored "threads" that join the sections together, use the brush and colored paints to make strips across the fold of the card. Paint these in a pattern like yellow, red, purple, and green, or use any bright colors you like. Before changing colors, rinse the brush in the bowl of water and blot it dry on a paper towel.

7 When the card is dry, turn it over. Write a message on the inside right section of the card. If you want, glue a photo of you and the person who is leaving on the inside left section. The person will always remember you.

© 1999 Gary Braman

Culture Link

Batik from Java

Batik (pronounced bah-TEEK) is colorful material with beautiful designs. Batik means "drop" in Javanese. (Java is the most important island of Indonesia.) Wax is "dropped" or pressed onto cloth to make the designs. The cloth is then dyed, but the wax design stays white. More wax designs are made on the material and it is dyed again. Doing this over and over again creates eye-dazzling designs.

Breathtaking Beads
ANCiENT EGYPTiAN BEADS

People all over the world have used beads for a long time. Beads have been found in graves in Sumer, an ancient country of western Asia, and in tombs in ancient Egypt. People used beads as money, to show how rich or important they were, and as protection from evil spirits.

Many cultures use beads to create unique designs in their jewelry. Italian glass beads made on the island of Murano in Venice, Italy, are world famous for their patterned decorations. Venetian artists craft beautiful necklaces using these beads. The *Samburu* (pronounced sam-BOO-roo) women of eastern Africa wear high stacks of bead collars for dances and ceremonies.

The ancient Egyptians made jewelry with beads. They believed that being buried with jewelry would bring luck and protection from evil. Traditional Egyptian jewelry used charms and beads of different shapes and sizes made from semiprecious gems and clay. Some of the shapes represented animals found in the Egyptians' environment, such as fish, birds, and insects. The charms and beads created a unique pattern for each piece of jewelry.

You can make your own Egyptian bead necklace using dough or store-bought clay. Copy the design shown here or create your own.

Here's What You Need

- piece of scrap paper
- pencil
- homemade dough (recipe on page 1) or store-bought, self-hardening clay
- ruler
- craft paintbrush
- plastic-coated paper plate
- toothpicks and twist ties (the ones used on trash bags)
- acrylic or poster paint (several colors)
- small bowl of water
- paper towels
- empty egg carton
- clear acrylic spray sealer (optional—requires adult help)
- scissors
- yarn

Here's What You Do

1 Look at the bead shapes shown on page 23. On scrap paper, draw a few designs for your necklace using these shapes. Experiment with different patterns.

2 Follow the recipe on page 1 to make the dough, or follow the directions on the box if using store-bought clay. Make the bead shapes with the dough. Your beads should be about ¼ to ½ inch (.5 to 1.5 cm) thick and ½ to 1 inch (1.5 to 2.5 cm) long. You will need about 8 to 12 beads, depending on their size and your design.

Bead Shapes

cube

round

triangle

tube

disk

pyramid

oval

teardrop

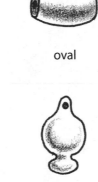

—— charms ——

3 Poke a hole all the way through each bead, using the blunt end of the paintbrush. Make sure the hole is big enough for stringing.

4 Place the beads on the paper plate. Let your dough beads air-dry on the plate about 5 days until very hard. Turn the beads over each day so all sides dry. For drying store-bought clay, follow the directions on the box. If the holes start to close, open them with the blunt end of the paintbrush.

smART tip

Don't want to wait 5 days? You can bake your dough beads, following the directions on pages 1–2.

5 To paint your beads, stick a twist tie or a few toothpicks (you'll need a few if the holes are big) through each bead hole. Hold the twist tie or toothpicks while you paint each bead. Paint the whole bead one color. You can paint each bead a different color. Remember to rinse the brush in the bowl of water and blot it dry on a paper towel before changing colors.

6 To dry, lay each bead (still in twist tie or toothpicks) across the egg sections of the egg carton. Or poke tiny holes in the egg carton and stick the twist ties or toothpicks in the holes. Let dry about 1 hour.

Culture Link

Peruvian Beads

The native Indians of Peru, a country in western South America, make ceramic, stone, and metal beads that are painted by hand in traditional designs. The unique beads are made into necklaces and other jewelry to sell to tourists who visit Peru. Many beads are sold to buyers, who then sell the beads in their bead shops so people can make their own necklaces.

7 Now you can paint designs on the beads if you like. Be creative! Let the paint dry completely. You can spray an acrylic sealer on the beads. This will help protect your beads. *Always use spray sealer outside with the help of an adult!* Let the sealer dry completely.

8 Cut a strand of yarn about 36 inches (92 cm) long. String your beads when they are dry. If you have a little trouble sticking the yarn through the holes, use a toothpick to push the yarn through the hole. Tie the ends of the yarn together in a tight knot.

PART TWO

Never Forget

There are so many things to remember: homework, music lessons, softball practice, karate forms, and what you did on your last vacation. How does a busy kid keep track of everything? You could write a list, keep a diary, use a computer, make a videotape, or take photographs to help you remember. But how did people keep records before things like computers existed?

People everywhere have always kept track of important things in their lives for all kinds of reasons. It wasn't always easy, but people all over the world found interesting ways. American Indians kept records on birch bark by drawing pictures that contained the information. Indian grandmothers kept track of how many grandchildren they had by making marks on a stone. These cultures and many others did it without writing!

In this section, you will experience record-keeping activities from different cultures that may help you remember the important things in your life.

Keeping Track
INCAN QUIPU

Many cultures have kept track of important events in their lives by using objects. The Inuit of Greenland used a piece of carved wood with seven holes as a weekly calendar. A wooden peg was moved from hole to hole as the days changed. The Haida Indians of the Queen Charlotte islands, in British Columbia, Canada, kept records of foreign visitors and sea captains with whom they traded by carving stone figures of them.

Another culture that had an interesting way of keeping track were the Incas. The Incas, the native people of Peru, ruled the largest empire in the Americas until they were conquered by the Spanish explorer Francisco Pizarro in 1532. During their rule, the Incas built cities high in the Andes Mountains and made beautiful gold jewelry, statues, and masks. They had a form of writing that used symbols called **ideographs** (graphic symbols that are used to express ideas), but they didn't use these to record important information.

So how did they keep track of things without writing them down? They invented a method called *quipu* (pronounced KEE-pooh). By making different kinds of knots on hundreds of different colored strings, they knew how many people were in the empire, how many new births and deaths there were each year, how much food was in storage, how many animals people owned, and many other things. Only certain people learned to do quipu.

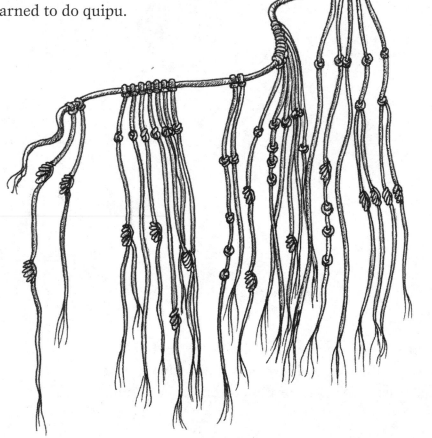

Now that you know how the Incas kept track, why not keep track of your life for two weeks. The next time your mom or dad says that you *never* eat your vegetables, you'll know by looking at your quipu tracking system.

Here's What You Need

- [ ] scissors
- [ ] yarn (6 different colors)
- [ ] ruler
- [ ] pencil
- [ ] cardboard (the inside of a cereal box or an old file folder)
- [ ] tape

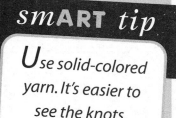

smART tip

Use solid-colored yarn. It's easier to see the knots.

Here's What You Do

1 Cut six pieces of yarn in different colors, each piece measuring 24 inches (61 cm) long.

2 Draw a rectangle on the cardboard 11 inches long by 2 inches wide (28 by 5 cm). Cut this out.

3 Tape one end of each piece of yarn to the cardboard. Space the yarns so they don't touch.

4 Above each piece of yarn, write something you want to keep track of. Here are some suggestions: number of sports you play, vegetables you eat, times you talk on the phone, A's you get in math, books you read, times you fight with your sister or brother, or anything you like.

5 Each time you do one of the activities listed, make a knot on the appropriate yarn. Always start at the top of the yarn and work your way down, adding a knot each time you do the activity. Remember to leave some space between knots and don't pull the knots too tightly.

6 At the end of two weeks, tally your results. Write the number next to each piece of yarn. What did you do the most? What did you do the least? If you need to make changes in your life (maybe read more books or stop fighting with your sister), just use your quipu tracking system to help you make those changes.

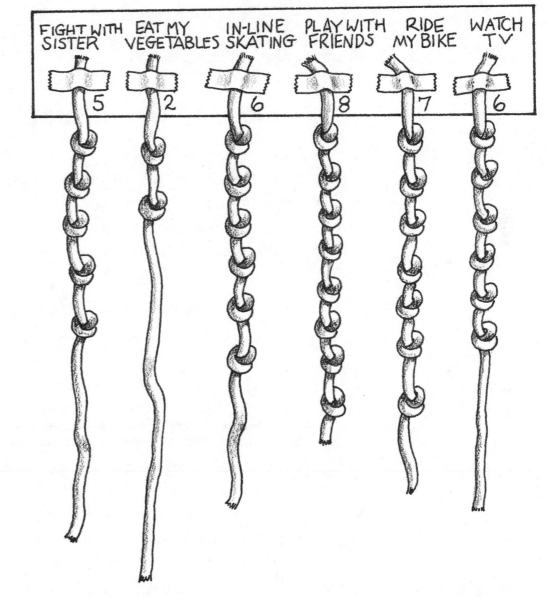

FIGHT WITH SISTER 5   EAT MY VEGETABLES 2   IN-LINE SKATING 6   PLAY WITH FRIENDS 8   RIDE MY BIKE 7   WATCH TV 6

Mayan Record Keeping

The ancient Maya, the native Indians who lived in southern Mexico and what is now Belize, Guatemala, and Honduras, also had an interesting tracking system. They kept accurate records using these pictures to represent numbers:

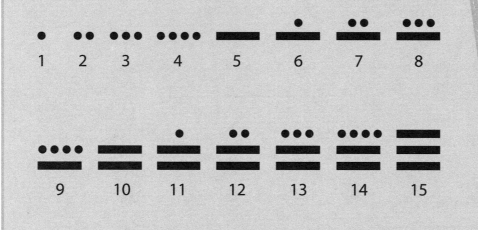

What do you think 16 would look like?

if These Walls Could Talk!
PREHISTORIC CAVE PAINTING

Thousands of years ago, prehistoric people painted pictures on cave walls and rock surfaces. These pictures showed different seasons, people working together, their handprints, and hunting animals. Some of the most famous paintings are found in the *Chauvet* (pronounced show-VEH) and *Lascaux* (pronounced lass-CO) caves in France. One of the oldest paintings, found in Spain, shows a figure of a person using a bow and arrow. Rock art from the desert in Jordan shows a herd of camels with their babies. These early forms of visual communication help us understand how prehistoric people lived, because their art recorded their life stories.

Prehistoric people painted with their fingers and with brushes made from animal hair and **reeds** (hollow stems of tall grasses). They spray-painted by blowing paint through a hollow reed.

How have these cave paintings lasted for so long? The temperature and climate inside a cave stays about the same all year. There is no rain or snow in the cave to wear down the paintings. This constant condition has helped to protect the paintings.

You don't need a cave to make a cave painting. A paper grocery bag works great! You can copy the record-keeping art of prehistoric people and make your handprints. You can also add some fingerprints and prehistoric symbols.

Here's What You Do

1 Draw a 12-by-17 inch (31-by-43 cm) rectangle on the bag and cut it out. To give the paper a jagged, cavelike look, carefully tear off small pieces along each edge of the rectangle.

2 Crinkle the paper into a loose ball, then open it and lay it flat. Place your left hand on the left side of the paper. Trace your hand lightly with the pencil, starting and ending at your wrist. Do the same for your right hand on the right side of the paper.

Here's What You Need

- [ ] pencil
- [ ] ruler
- [ ] brown paper bag (from the grocery store)
- [ ] scissors
- [ ] craft paintbrush
- [ ] acrylic or poster paint (about 4 different colors)
- [ ] small bowl of water
- [ ] paper towels

art choice Prehistoric artists made their own paint from soil. Because of the minerals in the soil, they could make black, brown, red, and yellow paint. You can use their colors for your painting, or choose different ones.

3 Paint over the outline of your hands with one color of paint.

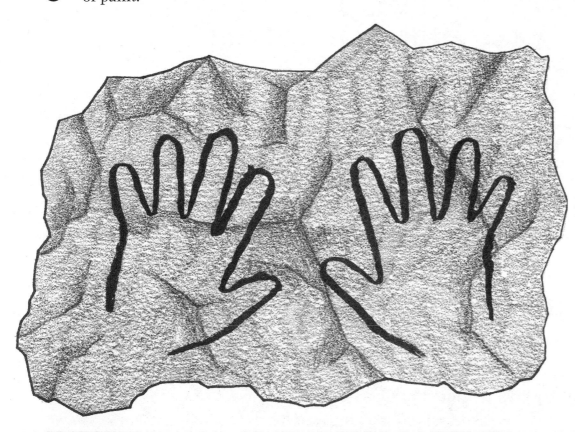

4 Now add some thumb- and fingerprints. Brush a little paint on your thumb or fingertip and press the paint onto the paper. Remember to rinse the brush in the bowl of water and blot it dry on a paper towel before changing colors.

5 Add some prehistoric symbols. Paint these with the brush.

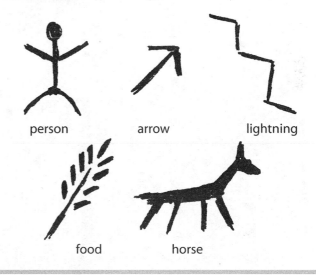

person   arrow   lightning

food   horse

6 Let your picture dry completely.

© 1997 Hurst Gallery

Culture Link

Sarcophagus Picture

The ancient Egyptians painted picture stories on the walls of tombs and on stone coffins called **sarcophagi.** Many of these picture stories told about traveling to another world after death. The sarcophagus picture shown here depicts *Qebsennuef* (pronounced keb-eh-SEN-o-wef), protector of the intestines, and *Duamutef* (pronounced due-ah-MO-tef), protector of the stomach.

The Storyteller
PUEBLO STORYTELLER FiGURE

Historians believe that all cultures have used storytelling to pass on information. Aboriginal storytellers from Australia tell of a "dreamtime," a time of their ancestors and the creation of the world. African slaves in America passed on their African heritage to their children through storytelling.

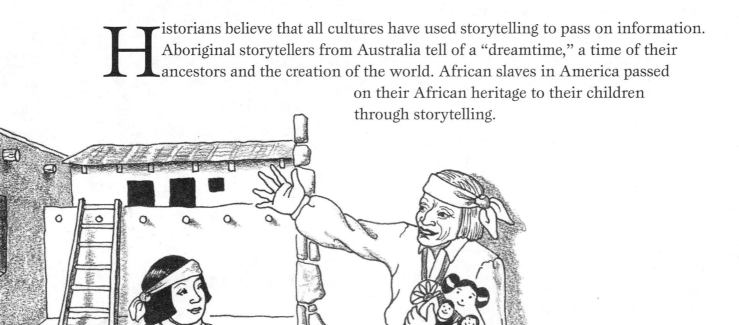

More than a thousand years ago, the ancestors of the Pueblo Indians, the Anasazi, lived in what is now the southwestern United States. They had no written language. Parents and grandparents used storytelling to pass on traditional legends about their people and their lives. One group of Pueblo Indians, the Cochiti, who live in New Mexico along the Rio Grande, continue to use storytelling even though they now have a written language. To help tell their stories, they use clay figures called Pueblo Storytellers. The Cochiti potters make the Storytellers in the same way their ancestors did, using colored clay from the earth. They make paints from plants and clay, and they fire the figures in homemade kilns.

The Pueblo Storyteller was and still is an important part of the Pueblo culture. Most of the figures look like a favorite grandmother or grandfather holding children on their laps who are listening to the stories.

You can make your own clay storyteller in the style of the Cochiti potters and start your own family storytelling tradition. Ask your grandparents to tell you stories about when they were young. Then you will have a record of your own culture and family history.

Here's What You Need

- [ ] homemade dough (recipe on page 1) or store-bought, self-hardening clay
- [ ] ruler
- [ ] small bowl of water
- [ ] plastic-coated paper plate
- [ ] acrylic or poster paint
- [ ] craft paintbrush
- [ ] toothpicks
- [ ] clear acrylic spray sealer (optional—requires adult help)

Here's What You Do

1 Follow the recipe on page 1 to make the dough, or follow the directions on the box if using store-bought clay. Roll a piece of dough into a ball about 2 to 3 inches (5 to 8 cm) in diameter. Roll the ball into a thick tube about 3 inches (8 cm) long.

2 Make the neck area by squeezing in the tube about one-third of the way down from the top. Mold the top third of the tube into a ball for the head. Shape the rest of the tube into the body, smoothing all edges. Your storyteller can stand or sit. To make it stand, flatten the bottom of the tube. You don't need to make legs. To make the storyteller sit, bend the bottom part of the tube into

Squeeze in neck area of dough

Flatten bottom for standing figure

Bend bottom part of figure into sitting position, then shape into 2 legs

a sitting position as shown, shaping the bottom into two legs.

3 Roll two small tubes of dough for the arms. Attach the arms and smooth all edges.

4 To make a few children, use a small piece of dough for each child. Shape each piece of dough into a tube. Shape the top of each tube into a head. Press the children onto the body of the storyteller. Smooth the edges of each child into the body of the storyteller.

smART tip

Before you attach the storyteller's arms and children, moisten the spot where you want them to go with a little water.

smART tip

Don't want to wait 5 days? You can bake your dough storyteller, following the directions on pages 1–2.

5 Let your dough storyteller air-dry on the paper plate about 5 days until very hard. For drying store-bought clay, follow the directions on the box. Turn the figure over each day so all sides dry.

6 When the figure is dry and hard, paint on a face and clothes, using a paintbrush. Use a toothpick to dot on the paint for eyes, nose, and mouth. Let the paint dry completely.

7 You can spray your storyteller with clear acrylic sealer. This will help protect your storyteller. *Always use sealer outside with the help of an adult!* Let the sealer dry completely.

Bamboo Strip Book
CHINESE BAMBOO STRIP BOOK

It's hard to imagine a time when people didn't have books. The earliest humans had to paint pictures on cave walls. Later cultures used stone or clay tablets. The ancient Egyptians may have been the first people to make books by writing on scrolls made of **papyrus** (a grasslike plant whose stems are used as a writing material). The ancient Greeks are credited with making the first bound book, which had wooden boards for the covers.

The first people in China to leave written records lived during the Shang dynasty, from about 1766 to 1122 B.C. Writers made Chinese characters on strips of **bamboo** (a tropical woody grass with hard stems). Using a brush and ink, the writers started at the top of the strip and worked their way to the bottom. When there were enough strips to make into a book, the strips were put in order, with the first strip on the right and the last on the left. Then the strips were tied together with silk string or leather strips. The book could be rolled up for easy carrying.

Unfortunately, most bamboo strip books and written records decayed over time. Very few records about this period in Chinese history exist today. In A.D. 105, the Chinese invented paper and no longer needed to use bamboo to make books.

It's easy to make your own bamboo strip book using craft sticks instead of real bamboo.

Here's What You Need

- glue
- 12 or more wooden craft sticks
- 8½-by-11-inch (21.5-by-28-cm) sheet of paper
- pencil
- small-bristle craft paintbrush
- black acrylic paint
- fine-tip permanent marker (optional)
- small piece of paper
- scissors

smART tip

Rest your hand on a piece of paper as you write so you don't smear the finished sticks.

Here's What You Do

1 Since bamboo strip books told of Chinese life, why not record one important event in your life on your bamboo strip book. It should be about something you want to remember forever. Did you travel to another continent, get your black belt in karate, or win a contest you entered? Think about it.

2 Glue the wooden sticks in a row on the paper.

3 While you're waiting for the glue to dry, write your important event on the paper. You can start like this: "Something I will always remember is . . ." Don't forget to record the date your event took place.

4 *Print* your important event on the sticks. Use the brush and paint (like the Chinese). You can do it the way bamboo strip books were written—top to bottom, right to left—as shown. Start at the top of the right stick. When you get to the bottom of that stick, go to the top of the next stick. Continue until you are finished. Remember to leave a space between words.

If you don't want to use a paintbrush to write on the sticks, use the permanent marker.

5 If you need more sticks, glue them on the paper. After you finish recording your event, cut around the outside of your bamboo strip book to get rid of the extra paper. Now an important event in your life has been recorded. Read your bamboo strip book to someone.

Write your important event on paper first

something I will always remember is our trip to the Statue of Liberty in February 1998

Use paintbrush or permanent marker

Glue the sticks in a row on the paper

Ledger Book

The Plains Indians of North America painted picture stories on buffalo hides and rocks. When the white settlers moved in, the Indians traded things the white people needed, like buckskin clothes and food, for horses, guns, and ledger paper. The ledger paper gave many American Indians another surface on which to paint picture stories. Some American Indians continue this tradition today.

© 1998 Hurst Gallery

PART THREE

Good Luck Always

Good-luck charms can look very different in different parts of the world. They might take the shape of a rabbit's foot, a penny, a stone sculpture, or a four-leaf clover. Some people believe that if they carry the object with them, it will bring them luck. In Tibet, a region of southwestern China, people wear medicine bracelets made of copper, brass, and white metal because they believe it will help keep their bodies healthy and in balance with nature. A charm can also be something a person does. Kids in Italy touch metal to bring them luck.

No one knows if good-luck charms really work, but people from all cultures have used and still use these objects. Many people believe charms have the power to protect, can bring luck, may keep bad things from happening, and bring good health. Whatever the reason, good-luck charms are fun to use.

The activities in this section show how different cultures have used charms. Who knows, maybe one of these will bring you luck!

Goodwill Message Flag
TiBETAN PRAYER FLAG

Many people around the world believe they can become better people by helping others and doing good deeds. Mother Teresa, who died in 1997, and her fellow **nuns** (women who belong to a religious order) have devoted their lives to caring for the sick in Calcutta, India. Buddhist monks in Nepal, a country in Asia next door to India, chant prayers every day, hoping to make the world a better place.

In Tibet, many Buddhists use a prayer wheel to help themselves and others. People write prayers on small pieces of paper and put them inside the prayer wheel. When they spin the wheel, the prayers are sent out into the world for all people.

Another way Tibetans improve themselves and do good for others is to make prayer flags. Tibetans dye pieces of cloth in colors that represent natural elements, such as blue for sky, white for clouds, red for fire, green for water, and yellow for earth. When the cloth flags are dry, someone writes prayers or special messages on each. The flags are linked following a color pattern of blue, white, red, green, and yellow. Since the flags represent the voice of God, they must be attached to a high place, such as the roof of a house or a bridge. Each time the wind blows and the flags flap in the breeze, the prayers or messages are sent out into the world.

You can make a goodwill message flag that will send your special message out into the world.

Here's What You Do

1 Think about the message you want to send that may help others. Write your message on scrap paper. Start with "I wish . . ." Here are some suggestions: I wish there were no more wars in the world, I wish everyone had enough food to eat, I wish clean air and water for the earth. Or write anything else that is important to you. Make sure the message is a complete sentence.

2 Draw a square on the pillowcase that is about 15 by 15 inches (38 by 38 cm). Cut this out with the pinking shears so the edges won't **fray** (wear away). If you use a handkerchief, you won't need to cut it.

Here's What You Need

- pencil
- scrap paper
- ruler
- clean white cloth
- pinking shears or scissors
- masking tape
- cardboard
- permanent colored markers

smART tip

Use a clean handkerchief or an old pillowcase.

3 Tape the cloth or handkerchief to the cardboard. Write your message in the center of the cloth with the markers.

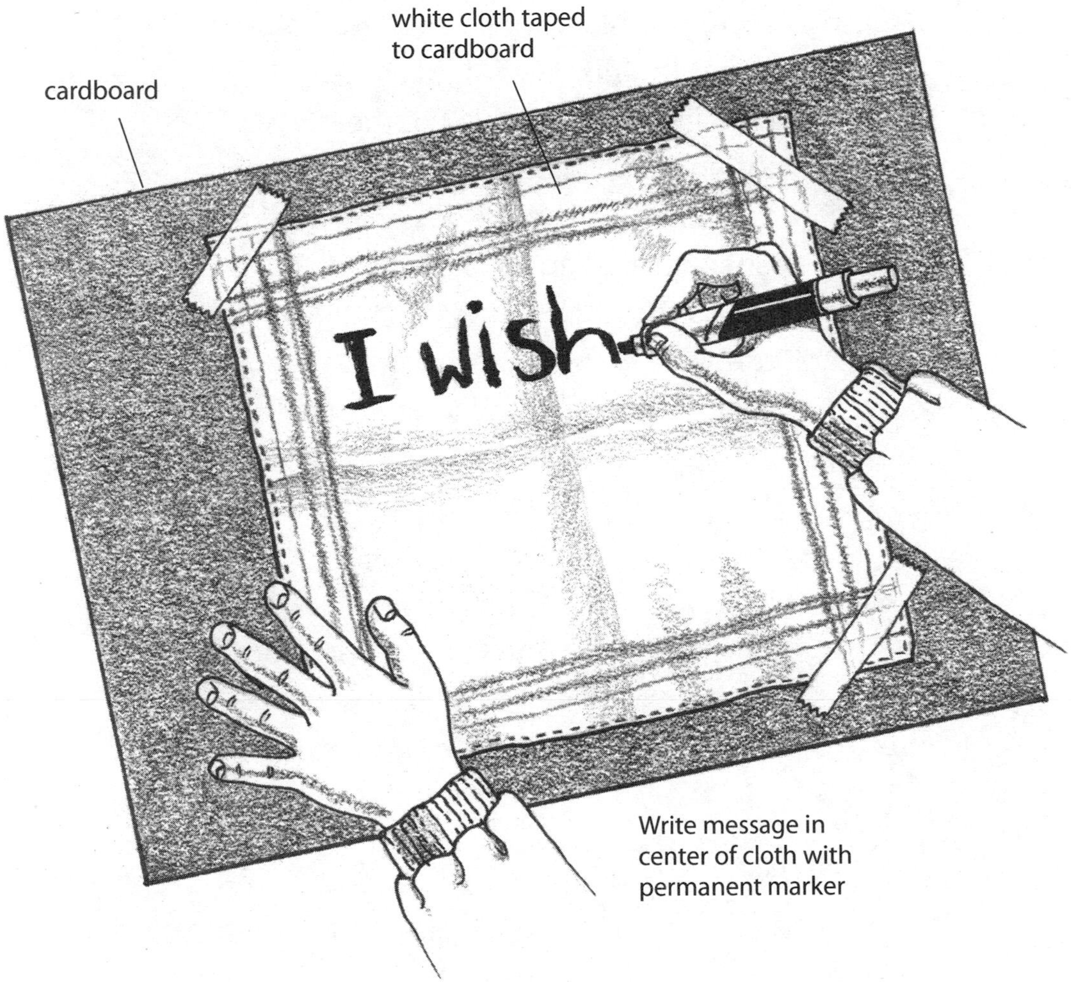

cardboard

white cloth taped to cardboard

I wish

Write message in center of cloth with permanent marker

4 Use your colored markers to decorate the border of your flag with Tibetan *dZi* (pronounced zee) bead designs. Tibetan *dZi* beads, found in the fields by farmers, have interesting patterns of lines and circles naturally carved on their surfaces. The beads are believed to have super-natural powers. Here are some of the designs that have been found on *dZi* beads:

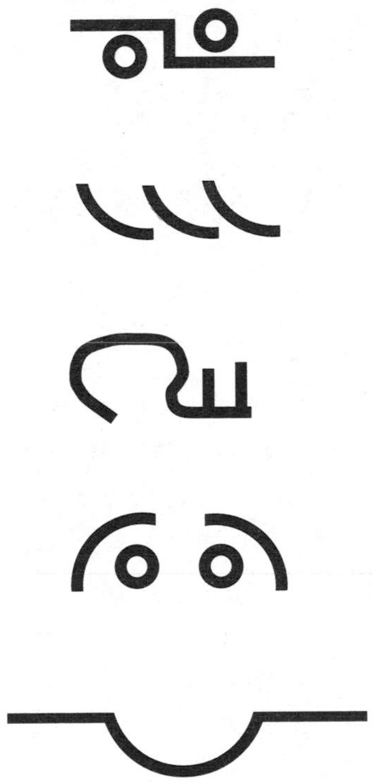

I wish people would realize how important the rainforest is.

5 Allow your flag to dry for 24 hours, then hang it. *Ask an adult for help.* You could hang it out your bedroom window, from a tree, fence, or clothesline, or any other place you like. Then watch your flag blow in the breeze as your goodwill message goes out into the world.

Culture Link

Thai *Krathong*

Each year in November, during a festival called *Loi Krathong* (pronounced loy crah-TONG), people in Thailand, a country in Southeast Asia, make floating flower boats called *krathongs*. Traditionally, the *krathongs* were made from folded banana leaves and shaped to look like an open lotus blossom. Today, banana leaves are still used, but people use other materials such as paper, Styrofoam, and flowers. Incense sticks, flowers, and a candle are placed in the center of the *krathong*. People float their *krathongs* in a stream and make a wish that all of their sins will be carried away by the water spirits.

Hei Tiki Pendant

MAORI HEI TIKI

Many cultures use **fetishes** (objects believed to have magical or spiritual powers) to bring them luck. The Otomí Indians of San Pablito, a mountainous village in central Mexico, hang cut-paper figures of humans and animals in their houses. In ancient Egypt, many people wore as a pendant a stone scarab, or beetle, which symbolized immortality.

The *Maori* (pronounced MOW-ree) are the native people of New Zealand, who traveled there in great canoes more than 600 years ago. Like many other cultures, they believe that charms have magical powers. One charm used by the Maori is a pendant called the *hei tiki* (pronounced hay TEE-kee). Hei means "hung" and tiki means "figure." The hei tiki is carved from **nephrite** (a type of jade that is white to dark green in color). The hei tiki stays in the family forever, passed down from one generation to the next.

Each hei tiki has its own special look because the figure reminds the carver of a certain spirit. It is believed that the spirit will live in the figure and protect its owner from harm.

You can make your hei tiki pendant out of dough or store-bought clay and paint it green to look like jade. Maybe when you wear your hei tiki you will feel safe, too.

Here's What You Need

- [ ] homemade dough (recipe on page 1) or store-bought, self-hardening clay
- [ ] ruler
- [ ] small bowl of water
- [ ] craft paintbrush
- [ ] plastic-coated paper plate
- [ ] acrylic or poster paint (green and several other colors)
- [ ] paper towels
- [ ] clear acrylic spray sealer (optional—requires adult help)
- [ ] scissors
- [ ] yarn

Here's What You Do

1 Follow the recipe on page 1 to make the dough, or follow the directions on the box if using store-bought clay. Shape a piece of dough into a rectangle about 3 inches long by 1½ inches wide (8 by 4 cm). Gently flatten the dough to about ¼ inch (.5 cm) thick.

2 Shape the rectangle into a hei tiki body. Smooth all edges.

3 Use more dough to make four small round balls for the nose, eyes, and mouth. Before you put on the eyes, moisten the area of the body with a little water.

4 For the nose and mouth, roll the remaining two balls into thin snakes. Moisten the area and attach.

5 Use the blunt end of the paintbrush to poke holes in the eyes and mouth, and to add detail as shown.

Shape hei tiki as shown

Use 4 small balls of dough to make the eyes, nose, and mouth

Use the blunt end of a paintbrush to make holes and add some detail

art choice

Many Maori hei tikis have tilted heads with open mouths or tongues that stick out. You can sculpt your hei tiki as the Maori do, or make up your own design.

6 About ¼ inch (.5 cm) down from the top of the head, poke a small hole through the dough with the blunt end of the paintbrush for the yarn to go through.

7 Let your dough hei tiki air-dry on a paper plate about 5 days until very hard. For drying store-bought clay, follow the directions on the box. Turn the figure over every day so all sides dry. If the holes start to close up, open them with the blunt end of the paintbrush.

8 Paint your hei tiki green to look like jade, or choose your favorite color. You can paint the eyes and mouth a different color. Remember to rinse the brush in the bowl of water and blot it dry on a paper towel before changing colors. Paint one side of the hei tiki first and let it dry about 1 hour. Then paint the other side. Let the paint dry completely.

smART tip

Don't want to wait 5 days? You can bake your dough hei tiki, following the directions on pages 1–2.

9 You can spray your hei tiki with acrylic spray sealer to help protect it. *Always use spray sealer outside with the help of an adult!* Let the sealer dry completely.

10 Cut a strand of yarn about 30 inches (76 cm) long. Put it through the hole and tie the ends together in a tight knot. Your hei tiki is ready to wear.

Thai Spirit House

The Daily Planet Catalog

In Thailand, many people have a spirit house outside their own house. It is believed that a guardian spirit lives in the spirit house and will protect the people's home. People put food, candles, and flowers around the spirit house as an offering to the spirit.

Arctic Paperweight
iNUiT ANiMAL SCULPTURE

To take a piece of wood or marble and carve it into an animal or other sculpture is a true art. People have been carving since the beginning of time. The Zuni, one of the largest Pueblo tribes of the American Southwest, are famous for their fetish carvings. The bear carving is an important fetish for its healing powers. In Ghana, in western Africa, the

Asante carve wooden *akua'ba* (pronounced ah-KWAH-bah) dolls for girls so that they will have beautiful children someday.

The Inuit, who live along the cold Arctic coast, carve sculptures from stone, driftwood, and ivory, which comes from walrus tusks. They carve likenesses of humans and familiar animals, such as seals, walruses, polar bears, birds, and whales.

Inuit are hunters, and they probably first carved animal figures as a way of honoring the animals they hunted. Early hunters believed these carved objects were magical and would bring them luck.

The Yupik of St. Lawrence Island in the Bering Sea use whalebone for their carvings. Every carver develops his own style, which is never copied by other carvers.

You can sculpt a paperweight in the likeness of an Arctic animal as the Yupik do, using homemade dough or store-bought clay instead of whalebone.

Here's What You Need

- [ ] homemade dough (recipe on page 1) or store-bought, self-hardening clay
- [ ] ruler
- [ ] paint brush
- [ ] plastic-coated paper plate
- [ ] acrylic or poster paints (several colors)
- [ ] small bowl of water
- [ ] paper towels
- [ ] clear acrylic spray sealer (optional—requires adult help)

Here's What You Do

1 Follow the recipe on page 1 to make the dough, or follow the directions on the box if using store-bought clay. Roll a piece of dough into a ball with a diameter of about 2 to 3 inches (5 to 8 cm).

2 Choose an Arctic animal such as a polar bear, whale, bird, seal, or walrus. Shape your animal from the ball of dough.

3 Smooth the surface of your sculpture to get rid of any cracks. Add finishing touches, such as eyes or a whale's blowhole, by using the blunt end of the paintbrush.

art choice To sculpt in the Yupik style, use very little detail.

Don't want to wait 5 days? You can bake your dough Arctic paperweight, following the directions on pages 1–2.

4 Let your dough sculpture air-dry on the paper plate about 5 days until very hard. For drying store-bought clay, follow the directions on the box. Turn the animal over every day so all sides dry.

5 Paint the bottom or one of the sides of the sculpture first. Let the paint dry about 1 hour, then paint the other sides of your animal. Remember to rinse the brush in the bowl of water, then blot it dry on a paper towel before changing colors. Let the paint dry completely.

6 You can spray your Arctic paperweight with acrylic sealer to help protect it. *Always use spray sealer outside with the help of an adult!* Let the sealer dry completely.

Culture Link

Bolivian *Pachamama* Figures

Thousands of miles south of the Arctic, the native Indians of Bolivia also carve objects and animal figures from stone. (Bolivia is a country in the Andes Mountains in western South America.) Artists carve likenesses of such animals as llamas, condors, owls, lizards, and jaguars. Healers use the figures to ask *Pachamama* (pronounced POCK-ah-mama), or Mother Earth, to bring luck or help for a particular problem. A carving of a llama, for example, will help make sure there is plenty of food.

© 1999 Gary Braman

No Worries
GREEK WORRY BEADS

Worry, worry, worry. What's a kid to do today, with so many things to worry about? There's the math test, the basketball play-offs, the science project, the gymnastics tryouts, and a gazillion other things to make you worry. Well, don't worry! Kids all over the world worry just like you, but some have special ways of dealing with their worries.

Children in the highlands of Guatemala, in Central America, sleep away their worries with worry dolls. Each night before going to bed, the child tells a different worry to each doll. The dolls are then put under the child's pillow. Legend says that the dolls will take away the worries by morning.

In the Middle East and Greece, some people have an interesting way to deal with worries. They roll a string of beads around in their hand to relieve tension. They call the beads "worry beads."

Where did worry beads come from? Some people believe worry beads came from prayer beads, which are beads or knots on a string that help people count their prayers. People who use worry beads say they really work.

It's easy to make your own worry beads with yarn and beads. (But you'll still have to study for that math test!)

Here's What You Do

1 Cut a strand of yarn about 21 inches (53 cm) long.

2 String the beads on the yarn. Leave about a 6-inch (15-cm) tail of yarn on both ends.

art choice

Greek worry beads are made from many different materials, such as wood, plastic, and ceramic. You can use either wooden or plastic beads, or use both kinds.

Here's What You Need

- yarn
- scissors
- 18 to 20 medium-size beads (wooden, plastic, or a combination)
- ruler

smART tip

Don't have any yarn? Use a shoelace or a piece of rawhide instead.

3 Tie the two ends of the yarn together in a knot close to the beads. Unravel the yarn ends. Trim the yarn ends a little shorter, if you like. With worry beads in hand, you can forget your worries.

Culture Link

Mexican Worry Stone

People in Mexico rub their worries away with worry stones. If they're feeling tense about something, they rub a flat, disk-shaped piece of marble—the worry stone—with their fingers. It is supposed to relieve tension by helping them focus on the stone, not their worries.

PART FOUR

Hold Everything

Every culture has had to come up with containers for holding their stuff, from an animal skull used as a bowl by the first humans to the colorful backpack you use to carry your schoolbooks.

There are woven baskets from the Amazon, carved wooden animal bowls from Thailand, and a canoe made from reeds of **totora** (a hollow-stemmed grass that grows around Lake Titicaca, which lies between Peru and Bolivia in South America). Each culture crafts its containers using materials found in its unique environment. A gourd grown in Africa is carved into a useful bowl. A piece of wood becomes a simple yet elegant Shaker box. (The **Shakers** were members of a Christian religious group who originally came from England and settled in North America in the 1700s.) The term *Shaker* refers to the style in which the object was made—simple, functional, and well crafted.

Each culture has interesting ways of decorating its containers. In Jalisco, a state in western Mexico, folk artists paint ceramic containers to look like regional fruits. A sacred bag used by a Yoruba holy man from Nigeria, a country in western Africa, is decorated with hundreds of tiny beads.

You will have fun making and decorating all of the containers in this section.

The "Oops" Basket
ZULU WOVEN BASKET

Baskets woven from materials found in the environment, such as grasses, vines, leaves, and bark, have been used by almost every culture in the world. They help make work easier and are great for storage, but they are also a form of artistic expression. Traditional Scottish baskets have a sturdy design using strips of willow. Sweet-grass baskets made by descendants of the slaves who were brought to America from western Africa have color woven into them. Today, some people use baskets to decorate their homes.

In the *Hluhluwe* (pronounced shah-SHLEW-ee) area of *KwaZulu Natal* (pronounced wah-ZU-LU NAH-tahl), a province within the Republic of South Africa, village women weave beautiful baskets of palm and rush reed. The Zulu women teach their daughters, some as young as 5 years old, the traditional art of basket weaving. The children weave small baskets called "oops" baskets because sometimes they make mistakes as they weave. These baskets are great for holding nuts and candy.

You can weave a basket like the ones woven by the Zulu children. If you make a mistake, call it your "oops" basket. What special treasures will your basket hold?

Here's What You Need

- [ ] sharp scissors (requires adult help)
- [ ] clean plastic yogurt cup (or other small plastic cup)
- [ ] ruler
- [ ] yarn (three-colored variegated yarn works nicely)
- [ ] masking tape
- [ ] paper clip

Here's What You Do

1 You need sharp scissors for this first step, *so ask an adult for help.* Cut slits in the cup, about 3/4 inch (2 cm) apart, starting at the rim and cutting down the side. Be sure you stop before you cut into the bottom of the cup. These slits separate the cup into strips. *You must have an uneven number of strips.* The number you have will depend on the size of the cup. With most small plastic cups, you'll probably have about 11, 13, 15, or 17 strips.

2 Cut a strand of yarn about 7 yards (6 m) long. Insert the yarn between any two strips. Slide the yarn down to the bottom of the slit, leaving about a 1/2-inch (1.5-cm) piece of yarn inside the cup. Tape the yarn end to the inside of either strip.

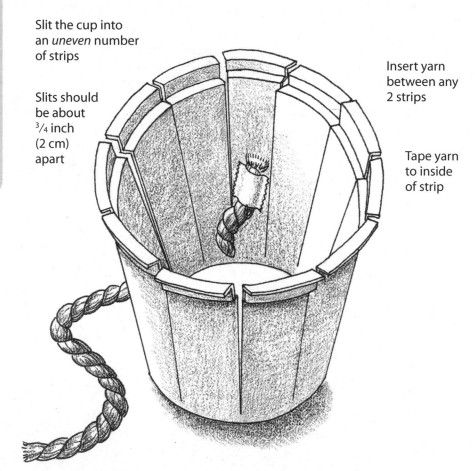

Slit the cup into an *uneven* number of strips

Slits should be about 3/4 inch (2 cm) apart

Insert yarn between any 2 strips

Tape yarn to inside of strip

3 Take the free end of the strand and start to weave it through the strips. Place it in front of the next strip to the right and then behind the strip after that. Repeat this pattern of *weave in front, weave behind* until the strand runs out. Push down each row close to the one before it. Tape the end of the strand to the inside of the nearest strip.

4 Cut another 7-yard (6-m) strand. Insert this strand in the *next* slit, after the slit where the first strand ended. Tape the yarn end to the inside of the nearest strip.

smART tip

*A*s you weave, don't pull the strand too tightly or the strips will start to pull in.

5 Continue to *weave in front, weave behind* until you reach the rim of the cup. Depending on the size of the cup, your strand may run out and you may need to cut more strands.

6 Make sure the yarn is secure between the strips at the rim and not popping out the top. After your last row, cut the yarn, leaving a 1-inch (2.5-cm) tail. Hide this yarn end on the inside of the basket. Use the paper clip to poke the yarn end into the weaving. This will keep the top row from unraveling.

Start new strand in *next* slit and continue weaving

Tape end of first strand to inside of strip

inside of cup

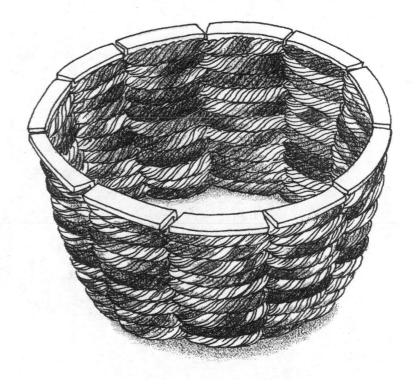

Culture Link

Paiute Beaded Basket

The Paiute (pronounced pie-YUTE) Indians of North America make beautiful baskets, which they decorate with glass beads. After making a coiled basket, the weaver covers the basket with beads that have been woven onto a net.

© 1992 Hurst Gallery

Depression-Era Scrap Bag
AMERICAN SACK CLOTH

Many people today recycle instead of throwing things away. A plastic egg carton makes a great container for paints. An old shoe box can become a storage container for toys. In the 1700s and 1800s, the Seminole Indians living in Florida knew about recycling. They cut scrap cloth into strips and pieced the strips together to make skirts, capes, dolls' clothes, and bags with beautiful designs.

In the 1930s, many families in the United States had to struggle to make a living. Because of problems with the U.S. economy, people lost their jobs and money and had very little food to eat.

This period became known as the Great Depression. Many people learned about recycling out of necessity.

During the Depression, women had to find inexpensive ways to make clothes for their children. They recycled cotton sacks that had held flour, animal feed, sugar, salt, or potatoes. Women cut and pieced together scraps from the sacks to make dresses, aprons, curtains, bedcovers, and pillowcases. It became so popular that sack companies started making sacks with designs, and sold booklets for 10¢ apiece that gave housewives tips on how to reuse the bags. Women went to "bag parties" to trade extra sacks for ones they needed. Sewing with sacks and scraps of cloth helped many families get by until times got better.

Find scraps of cloth around your house for your Depression-era scrap bag. This cloth container can hold money, jewelry, stickers, trading cards, or even small toys.

Here's What You Need

- [ ] scissors
- [ ] scraps of cloth
- [ ] ruler
- [ ] thread
- [ ] sewing needle
- [ ] straight pins
- [ ] pencil or chalk
- [ ] yarn
- [ ] small paper clip

Here's What You Do

1 Cut two pieces of cloth from the scraps, each measuring 8 inches long by 5½ inches wide (20.5 by 14 cm). Thread the needle and knot the ends of the thread together.

2 Put the right sides of the two pieces of cloth together. Pin them together around the edges except on one short side, which will be the top of your bag. Use the pencil or chalk to mark a ¼-inch (.5-cm) seam on the pinned edges.

3 Using a running stitch as shown, sew down one of the long edges, across the bottom edge, and up the other long edge, stopping 2 inches (5 cm) from the top. Sew over your last stitch three times to secure the thread, then cut the thread.

Running Stitch

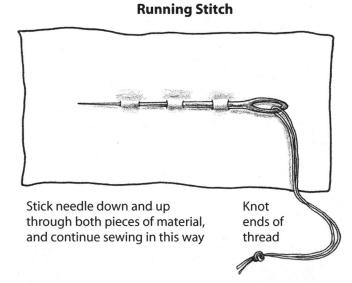

Stick needle down and up through both pieces of material, and continue sewing in this way

Knot ends of thread

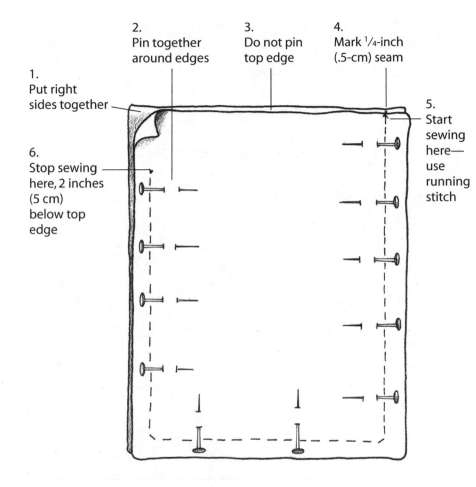

2.
Pin together around edges

3.
Do not pin top edge

4.
Mark ¼-inch (.5-cm) seam

1.
Put right sides together

5.
Start sewing here—use running stitch

6.
Stop sewing here, 2 inches (5 cm) below top edge

5 Cut a piece of yarn 24 inches (61 cm) long. Tie one end of the yarn to the paper clip. Push the paper clip through the opening in the hem at the top of the bag and work the yarn through the hem until you reach the opening on the other side. Remove the paper clip. Knot the ends of the yarn together.

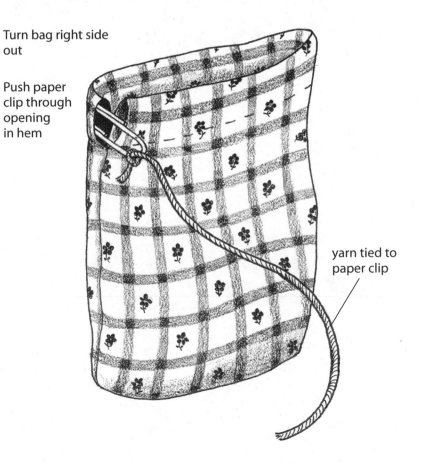

Turn bag right side out

Push paper clip through opening in hem

yarn tied to paper clip

4 Fold over 1 inch (2.5 cm) of the top edge and pin it in place. This is the hem for the top of the bag. Sew this piece to the bag, leaving a ¼-inch (.5-cm) seam. Be sure *not* to sew through both sides of the bag. Turn the bag right side out and press the hem and seams flat with your fingers.

6 Now your bag is ready to hold your treasures. To close the bag, hold the top of the bag and gently pull the yarn.

Perfect Pottery
CHINESE MING VASE

It is impossible to know who made the first piece of pottery, but we know that prehistoric people shaped clay from the earth into different useful objects. People needed containers like pots, bowls, pitchers, and cups for food, cooking, and storage.

Every culture leaves a distinctive mark on its pottery. Whether in the shape of the piece or in its design or color, each piece of pottery reflects the personality or identity of the culture who made it. An earthenware coffeepot from Sudan, a country in northeastern Africa, has little decoration but a useful shape. Ancient Andean cultures made interesting clay containers in the shape of chickens, frogs, people, and corncobs.

The period known as the Ming dynasty in China (A.D. 1368–1644) was a time of great cultural and artistic development. Potters made beautiful porcelain bowls, vases, and plates. They decorated their fine white porcelain with paintings of leaves, tree branches, dragons, animals, flowers, and people. Many of these images were painted in blue.

You will make a vase in the Chinese Ming dynasty style, using clay instead of the traditional porcelain.

Here's What You Need

- store-bought, self-hardening clay
- ruler
- plastic-coated paper plate
- acrylic or poster paint (white and blue)
- paintbrush
- clear acrylic spray sealer (optional—requires adult help)

Here's What You Do

1 Read the directions on the box of clay before you start.

2 Make a thick clay tube that measures 2 inches wide by 3 inches long (5 by 8 cm).

3 Stand the tube up and stick your finger into the center of the top of the tube. Push down as far as your finger will go without going through the bottom of the tube. Rotate your finger in the hole to help widen it.

4 Shape the tube into a vase by pressing the walls of the vase between your thumb and fingers. The walls of the vase should all be about the same thickness when you are finished.

5 Smooth the outside of the vase by gently rubbing the clay to get rid of any cracks. Some brands of clay crack less if you work with moist hands.

Create your own shape for your vase or copy one of these.

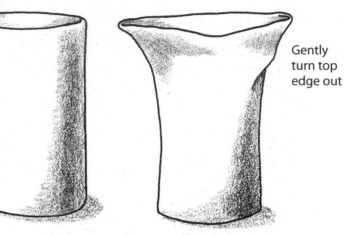

Keep sides straight

Gently turn top edge out

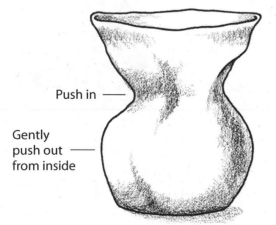

Push in

Gently push out from inside

6 Follow the directions on the box for drying and hardening the clay. For air-drying and hardening, place the vase on the paper plate. Turn the vase over now and then so that all sides dry and harden.

7 Paint the outside of your vase white unless you used white clay. Let the paint dry completely. Paint Ming dynasty designs on the vase in blue. Let the paint dry completely.

art choice

Here are some designs found on Ming dynasty porcelain. You can copy one of these or create your own.

8 You can spray the vase with acrylic sealer to help protect it. *Always use spray sealer outside with the help of an adult!* Let the sealer dry completely. Your vase is ready for flowers. *Make sure you don't put water in the vase. Use only dried flowers.*

Culture Link

Venetian Glass

Master glassmakers who live on the island of Murano in Venice, Italy, make beautiful glass vases and bottles with traditional designs. These Venetian glassmakers use the same techniques that were developed by the original master glassmakers in the eleventh century.

PART FIVE

Masters of Disguise

Kids in Canada and the United States disguise themselves with masks and costumes on October 31 for Halloween. On this scary day, it's fun to change your appearance and pretend you're someone else.

People in many other cultures change their appearance for special occasions. American Indians wear fancy costumes to dance at a **powwow** (a gathering of tribes where Indians can celebrate their culture). *Wodaabe* (pronounced wo-DAH-bee) men from the west African republic of Niger paint their faces to show beauty. Brides in China wear headdresses of flowers, feathers, pearls, butterflies, and beads. Japanese actors wear *Noh* (pronounced no) masks with exaggerated expressions so the audience will understand the emotions of the actor's character.

It's fun and magical to disguise yourself and be someone else, even if it's only for a little while. Have fun disguising yourself with the activities from many lands in this chapter.

What a Face!
SUDANESE FACE PAINTING

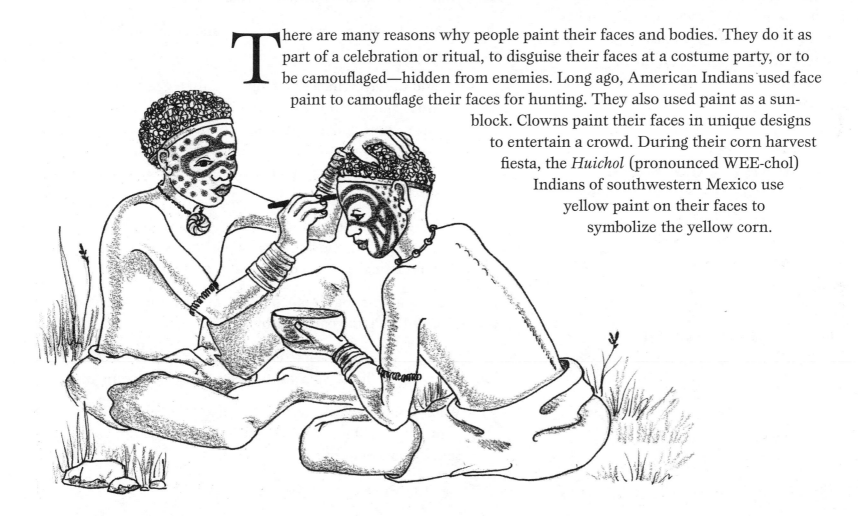

There are many reasons why people paint their faces and bodies. They do it as part of a celebration or ritual, to disguise their faces at a costume party, or to be camouflaged—hidden from enemies. Long ago, American Indians used face paint to camouflage their faces for hunting. They also used paint as a sunblock. Clowns paint their faces in unique designs to entertain a crowd. During their corn harvest fiesta, the *Huichol* (pronounced WEE-chol) Indians of southwestern Mexico use yellow paint on their faces to symbolize the yellow corn.

In the Nuba Mountains of Sudan, a country in northeastern Africa, Southeast Nuba men take great pride in painting elaborate designs on their faces. They must change the design every day. It is considered a challenge and a true art to create a new design each morning. If the man's design isn't very good, he starts over. Women are not allowed to paint designs on their faces, but may cover their faces with paint.

Face painting is fun to do. You can become anyone or anything you like with a few strokes of a brush.

Here's What You Need

- store-bought face paint (optional)
- for homemade face paint you'll need:
  - 2 teaspoons (10 ml) shortening
  - 2 1/2 teaspoons (12.5 ml) cornstarch
  - 1 teaspoon (5 ml) white flour
  - glycerine (available at drug stores)
  - eyedropper
  - food coloring
- cold cream
- paintbrush
- friend
- mirror (optional)

Here's What You Do

1 You can buy face paint at a craft, toy, or art store, or make your own by following these steps:

- Mix the shortening, cornstarch, and flour until it forms a paste.

- Add the glycerin, a few drops at a time. Start with four drops and stir. If the mixture doesn't spread easily, add one or two more drops. This mixture will not have the consistency of store-bought face paint. It is thicker, like icing for cake. The glycerin helps to make it easier to spread.

- Split the mixture into four small portions. Add a few drops of food coloring to each portion. Stir well. If you want to make more colors, make another batch.*

2 Smooth a little cold cream on your face before you paint it. This will help the paint wash off easily.

3 Start painting! It's best to do this with a friend, painting each other's faces. To paint your own face, use a mirror.

4 Wash your face before you go to bed. Never sleep with face paint on. It will mess up your sheets (yuck), get in your eyes (ouch), and clog your pores (gross).

* Reprinted by permission of Lands' End, Inc., Dodgeville, Wis. © 1998.

Read this! Never use any paint on your face except homemade face paint or paint you buy that is made for face painting. All other paints can cause rashes on your skin!

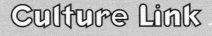

Culture Link

Designs from Other Cultures

People from many cultures paint interesting and unique designs on their faces. Here are a few designs from around the world.

Karo of Ethiopia

American Indian of Pacific Northwest

Huichol of Mexico

Marvelous Masks
ITALIAN CARNIVAL MASK

A mask can be magical. Put one on and suddenly you've become someone or something else. Masks can be made from materials such as cardboard, papier-mâché, plaster, cloth, and wood. Some people like to decorate their masks with feathers, animal hair, beads, paint and glitter, and small pieces of colored glass.

Some cultures, like the Inuit, believe that when a mask is worn, the wearer "becomes" the spirit that is represented by the mask. For others, a mask serves as a disguise at a party or parade. People wear masks at festivals and for religious ceremonies. Ancient cultures from Mexico, like the Toltecs, even put masks on mummies to protect them from evil in the afterlife.

Carnival in Venice, Italy, is a time when people celebrate the coming of spring by dressing in costumes, having parades, and going to parties and dances. But one of the most important things about carnival is to wear a mask. Many masks are handmade by artists who compete with one another to see who can create the most original mask. Some masks are fancy, with gold paint, glitter, and feathers. Others are huge papier-mâché masks that fit over the head. In the 1700s, the people of Venice put sticks on their masks and held the masks in front of their faces because their hairstyles were so big. It made more sense to hold the mask rather than put it over a big hairstyle.

You will make an Italian carnival half-mask with an attached stick like the ones people wear at carnival in Venice.

Here's What You Need

- [ ] pencil
- [ ] ruler
- [ ] firm piece of cardboard (from shoe box, cat food box, or cereal box)
- [ ] scissors (may require adult help)
- [ ] tape
- [ ] plastic straw
- [ ] glue

- [ ] decorations (any of these are good: feathers, glitter, paper confetti, aluminum foil, gold/silver stars, yarn, cotton balls, pipe cleaners, beads, and fake gems)
- [ ] paintbrush
- [ ] acrylic or poster paint
- [ ] small bowl of water
- [ ] paper towels

Here's What You Do

1 Draw a 9-by-7-inch (23-by-18-cm) rectangle on the cardboard. Cut this out. Fold the cardboard in half along the short edge. On the cardboard, draw one of the three half-mask shapes shown here. Be sure you start and end on the fold line. Cut out the shape, cutting through both layers of the cardboard. Do *not* cut along the fold line.

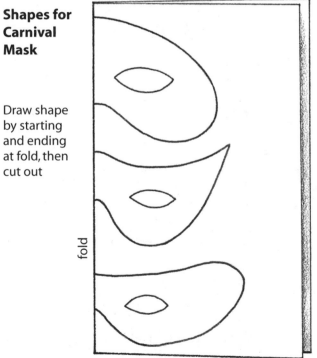

Shapes for Carnival Mask

Draw shape by starting and ending at fold, then cut out

fold

2 Unfold the mask shape. Draw eyes on the mask, then cut them out. *If the cardboard is very firm, you may need adult help cutting the eyeholes.* Hold the mask up to your face. Reshape the eyeholes if needed.

3 Tape the plastic straw to the *back* right or left side of the mask.

4 If you'd like to make a nose for your mask, use a scrap piece of cardboard. Cut out a triangle, fold it in half, then unfold it. Fold along the short bottom edge to make a flap. Cut the center of the flap to the fold. Glue the flaps to the inside of the mask. You may need to add tape for extra hold.

5 Before you paint your mask, get your decorations ready. Paint the mask any color you'd like. Remember to rinse the brush in the bowl of water, then blot it dry on a paper towel before changing colors. Before the paint dries completely, sprinkle on glitter, then put on the cut stars or any other decoration that will stick to the wet paint. Let the paint dry completely. Glue on remaining decorations. Let the glue dry completely.

smART tip

To attach feathers, poke a small hole in the mask using the scissors and stick the end of the feather in the hole. Tape the end to the back of the mask.

How to Make a Nose

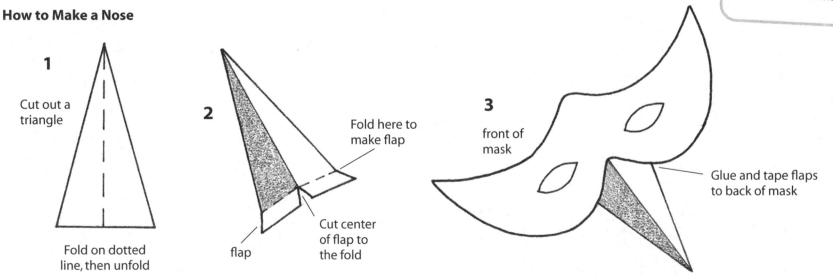

1 Cut out a triangle

Fold on dotted line, then unfold

2 Fold here to make flap

Cut center of flap to the fold

flap

3 front of mask

Glue and tape flaps to back of mask

6 Hold your mask in front of your face. Who or what have you become?

it's All on Your Head
AMAZONIAN INDIAN HEADDRESS

A headdress is a kind of decoration for your head. Headdresses come in all sizes, shapes, colors, and styles. One of the oldest kinds of headdress is the feather headdress. In addition to feathers, other decorations for headdresses include flowers, beads, bamboo, shells, precious gems, animal skins, and bells.

The *Maori* of New Zealand wear rare feathers in their hair for special occasions. These feathers have been passed down from their ancestors and are kept in boxes for safekeeping. In Sweden, many children wear a headdress of lingonberry leaves and candles on Saint Lucia's Day. The queen of England wears a crown made of gold and precious gems for royal ceremonies.

Amazonian Indians of northern South America wear feather headdresses for many ceremonies. Color is an important part of the headdress. A **shaman** (a person who acts as a communication link between humans and spirits) may wear a black-feathered headdress when the sun doesn't shine, and change to a scarlet macaw-feathered headdress to ask the sun to shine.

In this activity, you will make a traditional Amazonian Indian headdress. Think about the colors you want to use for your feather headdress and what those colors mean to you. Wear your headdress when you want to celebrate or whenever you like.

Here's What You Need

- 9-by-12-inch (23-by-30.5-cm) construction paper (a variety of colors)
- tape
- scissors
- pencil
- glue stick

Here's What You Do

1 Take one piece of construction paper and lay it on a table with the long sides on the top and bottom. Take the two top corners and bring them together. Put one corner over the other and tape them together. This makes a cone-shaped hat.

Bring top 2 corners of paper together, overlap, and tape

This is the back of the headdress

2 Cut paper feathers out of lots of different colors of construction paper. To make the feathers, fold the paper in half, long ends together. Draw about five to six oval-shaped feathers that are pointed at the top and bottom. Cut out the feathers, cutting through both layers of paper. Make small cuts along the curved sides of the feathers.

3 Starting at the bottom edge, glue a row of feathers all around the cone. Glue the next row a little above the first row so that the feathers overlap. Keep gluing feathers until the entire headdress is covered.

4 Glue a few feathers to the top of the headdress so that they stick straight up.

5 Try on your Amazonian Indian headdress.

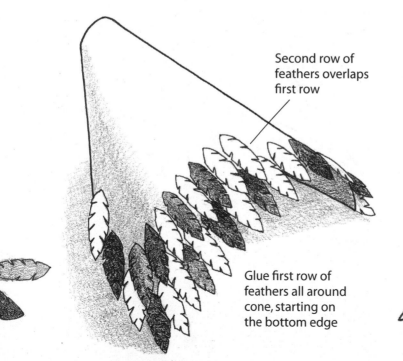

Second row of feathers overlaps first row

Glue first row of feathers all around cone, starting on the bottom edge

Micronesian Headdress

In the 1800s, very important men and women of Micronesia, a group of islands in the South Pacific, wore headdresses during royal ceremonies. These headdresses were made of porpoise teeth, shells, and coral disk beads strung on braided coconut fiber. The crowns were considered a mark of high status and wealth because the individual elements of the headdress could be used as currency.

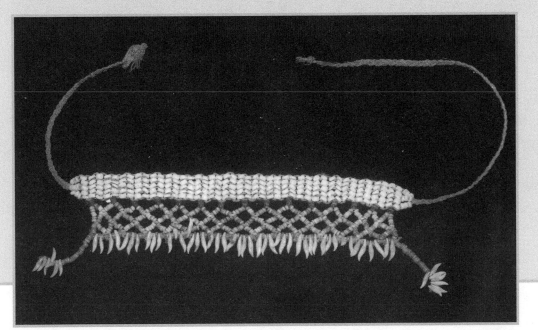

© 1998 Hurst Gallery

Body Deco
INDIAN ANKLE BRACELET

Each morning before you go out, you put on clothes, your watch, maybe a bracelet, necklace, or earrings. You make a statement with what you put on your body. It's a way of saying I'm cool, I'm comfortable, I'm on their team, or I'm going to a party!

Many cultures use body decoration. Hawaiian dancers wear grass skirts when they perform the traditional hula dance. In South Africa, young Zulu girls give their boyfriends "love letters" in the form of bead necklaces. The patterns and colors of the beads in the necklace communicate a message to the boyfriend.

In India, many brides have intricate designs painted on their hands and feet with **henna** (a natural reddish brown dye). For traditional Indian dances, women wear bell bracelets around their ankles.

You can make your own Indian ankle bracelet to wear whenever you feel like kicking up your heels.

Here's What You Need

- scissors
- plastic craft cord (used in jewelry making) or string, yarn, or shoelace
- ruler
- 1 package medium-size jingle bells (available at craft stores) or uncooked small pasta (wagon wheels, elbows, or ditalini) or buttons

Here's What You Do

1 Cut a piece of cord 24 inches (61 cm) long.

2 Thread the bells on the cord. Slide the bells to the middle section of the cord, leaving about 8 inches (20 cm) of cord on both ends.

3 Tie a knot on each cord end close to the bells so they don't slide off. Tie the bracelet around your ankle in a bow. Cut off any long pieces of cord.

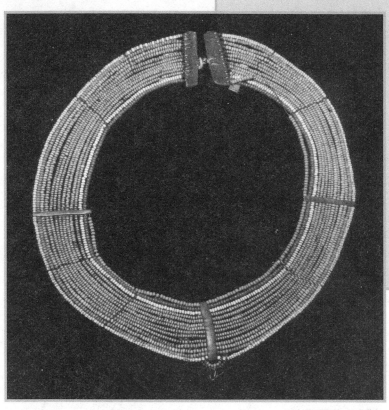

© 1998 Hurst Gallery

Beaded Collar

Masai women in Kenya, a country in eastern Africa, wear stiff beaded collars around their necks to let men know that they are available for marriage. Sometimes a woman has so many collars that she stacks them, one on top of the other.

PART SIX

It's Party Time

Everyone around the world enjoys a party. There are holidays like Christmas, May Day, Chinese New Year, *Hanukkah* (pronounced HON-uh-kah), and *Dewali* (pronounced dee-VAH-lee), and of course there are birthdays. Many celebrations are unique to a culture. Others are similar. But the kinds of things people do when they have a celebration, like sending invitations, decorating, playing music, and giving gifts, are common to all cultures.

Why not make up your own cultural celebration using some of the things from this book. Get your friends to help. The activities in this section will help you write an invitation, decorate your space, make a musical instrument, and wrap a gift in a unique way. Don't forget to wear some of the things you've made, such as your Amazonian headdress, Egyptian beads, Maori hei tiki necklace, or Sudanese face paint. Don't forget to have a really great time.

Come One, Come All
EARLY ENGLISH INVITATION

One of the first things you need to do if you want to have a celebration is to invite your friends by sending out invitations about the special day. These days, invitations are usually cards that include the reason for the celebration, the date, the time, the place, and any special instructions (like "wear masks!"). How did people make and send invitations long ago? When the Algonquin Indians of North America wanted to invite friends to dinner, they painted pictures on small blocks of wood that told of the event. Then runners delivered the message to the invited guests. The Aboriginal people of Australia carved marks on sticks and bark that contained information to invite someone to a special event or important meeting, or to announce the birth or death of a family member. Messengers then delivered the sticks.

During the 1600s in England, people didn't use carved sticks or blocks of wood for invitations. They wrote the message on large sheets of white paper, imprinting the first letter with a stamp. A messenger called a **page** (a young man who delivered messages or did errands) then delivered the invitation and usually waited for a response.

You can send an invitation to your friends to invite them to your cultural celebration, but you won't use a stick or block of wood. You'll design a card and make your own personal stamp with dough or clay.

Here's What You Need

- [ ] homemade dough (recipe on page 1) or store-bought, self-hardening clay
- [ ] ruler
- [ ] paintbrush
- [ ] plastic-coated paper plate
- [ ] scissors
- [ ] white construction paper
- [ ] poster or acrylic paints
- [ ] crayons, colored pencils, or markers
- [ ] envelopes (optional)
- [ ] postage stamps (optional)

Here's What You Do

1 Follow the recipe on page 1 to make the dough, or follow the directions on the box if using store-bought clay. To make your personalized stamp, shape the dough into a 2-by-2-inch (5-by-5-cm) block. The block should be at least 1 inch (2.5 cm) thick. With the blunt end of the paintbrush, deeply carve the initial of your first or last name into one of the flat surfaces of the dough. Let the dough stamp air-dry on the paper plate about 5 days until very hard. Turn the stamp over every day so all sides dry. Make sure your carved initial doesn't close up.

smART tip

Don't want to wait 5 days? You can bake your dough stamp, following the directions on pages 1–2.

2 For each card, cut a piece of paper that measures $5\frac{1}{2}$ by $8\frac{1}{2}$ inches (14 by 21.5 cm). Fold the piece of paper in half.

3 Make sure the fold of the card is at the left before you decorate it. First paint the carved initial any color you like, then press the painted stamp on the center of the front of the invitation. Let the paint dry completely.

4 Using crayons, markers, or colored pencils, decorate the border of your invitation with designs that represent different cultures. Give your celebration a name.

5 On the inside left section of the card, write a message about your celebration. Why not try writing it as a poem? Your message should give the person receiving the card information about the celebration.

6 On the inside right section of the card, write the date, time, and place for the celebration, along with your name and phone number so friends can call and let you know if they can come. And don't forget to remind them to wear their headdresses or maybe bring some food from another culture.

art choice **H**ere are some cultural designs you can use for decorating your invitation. Or create your own.

Celtic

African

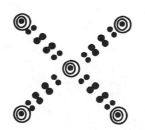

Aboriginal/Australian

7 You can either give the invitations to your friends or mail them.

Culture Link

Christmas Card

English artist John Callcott Horsley designed the first Christmas card in 1843. It looked like a modern-day postcard depicting a family. People enjoyed sending and receiving these greeting cards. For some people it was a way of "catching up" with family news, especially if they lived far away.

Light the Way
KOREAN PAPER LANTERNS

Party decorations in many cultures include fancy lights. People in Germany decorate their Christmas trees with lighted candles. In Egypt, children celebrate the birthday of the prophet Muhammad by saying prayers at the **mosque** (a place where Muslims pray), which is covered with beautiful colored lights. During the festival of Dewali, Hindus in India place rows of clay lamps on the roofs of their homes. Dewali means "rows of lighted lamps," and these lights are beautiful when they are lit up at night.

In Korea, people honor Buddha's birthday during a spring festival. Weeks before the festival they make lots of paper lanterns. The day before the festival, everyone decorates the temples by hanging the paper lanterns. In the evening, people walk through the streets carrying real lanterns and then leave them at the temples. It is a magnificent sight.

You can make paper lanterns for your celebration. Make a whole bunch and hang them everywhere.

Here's What You Need

- [ ] 9-by-12-inch (23-by-30.5-cm) construction paper
- [ ] scissors
- [ ] ruler
- [ ] glue stick
- [ ] glitter
- [ ] tape
- [ ] yarn or string

Here's What You Do

1 Fold the construction paper in half, long sides together. Cut 4 slits, each 3½ inches (9 cm) deep, evenly spaced, along the fold. Leave 1 inch (2.5 cm) of paper uncut at the open end.

2 Open the paper with the folded edge faceup and lay the paper flat. Rub small areas with glue, then sprinkle on glitter. You don't have to cover the entire lantern. Let the glue dry.

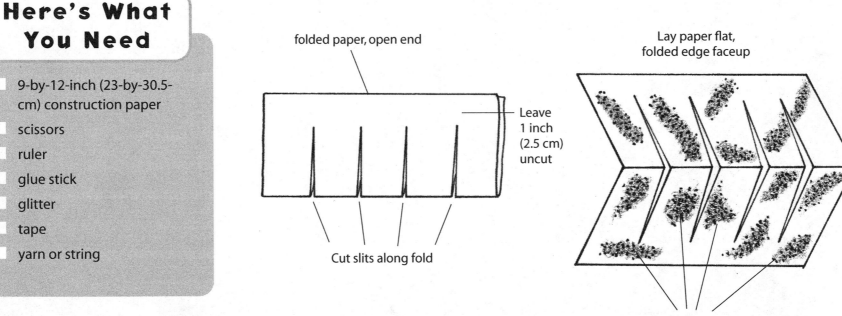

folded paper, open end

Leave 1 inch (2.5 cm) uncut

Cut slits along fold

Lay paper flat, folded edge faceup

glitter

3 Bring the two short edges of the paper together and secure with tape at each end. The strips should bend out. You can stand your lantern on a table, or hang it following the next step.

4 Cut a piece of yarn or string 12 inches (31 cm) long. Tape each end of the string to the inside of the lantern's top rim.
Hang your lantern.

Culture Link

The Lights of Kwanzaa

African Americans celebrate Kwanzaa from December 26 to January 1. The holiday is based on seven guiding principles (unity, self-determination, collective work and responsibility, cooperative economics, purpose, creativity, and faith), one for each day of Kwanzaa. It is a time for African Americans to reaffirm their heritage. One candle from the *kinara* (Swahili for candleholder for seven candles) is lit each night of Kwanzaa. The Swahili word *Imani,* carved on the *kinara,* stands for faith.

Making Music
CARIBBEAN ISLAND MARACAS

Music is an important part of many celebrations. Musical instruments can be found in all cultures around the world. *Castanets* (pronounced cass-tuh-NETS) from Spain are made from shells or hardwood and are clapped together with the fingers during the lively *flamenco* (pronounced flah-MENK-oh) dance. The Aboriginal people of Australia let termites help make their *didgeridoo* (pronounced didg-ur-ee-DOO). After an Aborigine buries a branch of **eucalyptus** (tall tree native to Australia), termites eat the soft wood inside, creating a hollow tube. The branch is then dug up, decorated, and played for special occasions by blowing through the top, open end.

The music of the Caribbean islands comes from a wonderful mix of cultures, including Indian, African, Spanish, French, British, and American. One instrument developed by the Indians before Columbus arrived is the maraca.

Indians such as the *Arawaks* (pronounced AH-rah-wahks) and the *Caribs* (KAR-ebz), who lived in the Caribbean islands, made maracas from hollow gourds that were filled with seeds. Today, maracas are still used. Many are painted with island scenes and designs. Two maracas are usually shaken together during a song or dance.

It's easy to make a pair of island maracas for your cultural celebration. You don't need a gourd. A plastic bottle works great.

Here's What You Need

- 2 plastic water bottles with caps, 20 fluid ounces (591 ml) or smaller
- paintbrush
- acrylic or poster paints
- small bowl of water
- paper towels
- clear acrylic spray sealer (optional—requires adult help)
- small stones, pasta, beads, or beans

Here's What You Do

1 Remove as much of the paper from the outside of the bottles as you can. Paint the bottles all one color or a few different colors. Remember to rinse the brush in the bowl of water, then blot it dry on a paper towel before changing colors. Let the first coat dry completely. Paint a second coat of the same colors and let it dry.

2 Paint island scenes or designs on the maracas. Paint palm trees, coconuts, the beach, the ocean, the sun, waves, or whatever you like. Let the paint dry completely.

3 You can spray your maracas with acrylic sealer to help protect them. *Always use spray sealer outside with the help of an adult!* Let the sealer dry completely.

smART tip

*K*eep the cap on the bottle while you paint so you can hold the bottle by the cap. It's a lot easier that way.

4 Fill each maraca about halfway with the beans, stones, pasta, or beads. Put on the caps, hold the maracas by the neck, and shake them.

Culture Link

Rain Stick

Another instrument that uses seeds to make beautiful music is the rain stick from Chile, a country in South America. To make a rain stick, native people clean the inside shell of a dead cactus, pound the thorns into the shell, fill the inside with seeds, then seal the ends. As the stick is turned, a rainlike sound is made by the seeds falling through the web of thorns.

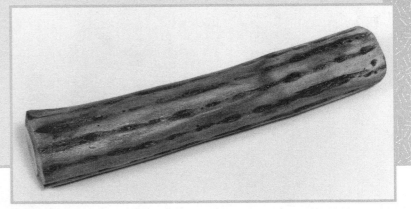

© 1999 Gary Braman

Give a Gift
JAPANESE MiZUHiKi

Gift giving is a custom shared by many cultures and is often a part of many celebrations. Most gifts are wrapped with fancy paper and tied with ribbons, or a gift bag is used. African American parents and children exchange gifts during Kwanzaa. During Purim, Jewish people give at least two kinds of food to friends based on the tradition of giving gifts to the poor. Many French children decorate handmade cards for their mothers on Mother's Day.

In Japan, people have an interesting way to decorate a gift. After the gift is wrapped, it is covered with many colored strings tied in beautiful knots. The strings are called *mizuhiki* (pronounced mih-zoo-HEE-kee), which means "water drawn," because of the way they were made long ago. Flax plants were soaked in water and thin fibers were pulled from the plant. Today, *mizuhiki* is made from strips of paper that are tightly twisted together. They can be tied into fancy knots or animal, plant, and fish designs. It is considered rude to give a gift that is not tied up properly. *Mizuhiki* string is also used to decorate envelopes.

Your gift envelope will be decorated with yarn. You can give the envelope, with something special inside, to friends who come to your cultural celebration.

Here's What You Need

- [ ] pencil
- [ ] scrap paper
- [ ] white envelope (card- or letter-size)
- [ ] scissors
- [ ] yarn (different colors)
- [ ] ruler
- [ ] glue stick
- [ ] damp paper towel

Here's What You Do

1 Practice drawing a few designs on the scrap paper. Then lightly draw a design on the front of the envelope with the pencil.

 **art choice** Use one of these designs or create your own.

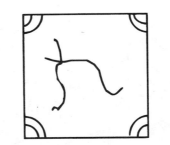
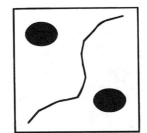

2 Cut a few strands of yarn, each about 12 inches (30 cm) long.

3 Using the edge of the glue stick, not the top flat part, rub glue over a 2-inch (5-cm) section of the design. Lay a strand of yarn over that section and gently press it down. Work in 2-inch (5-cm) sections until the entire design is covered. Cut off any extra pieces of yarn. Wipe your fingers on the damp paper towel often so they won't stick to the yarn.

4 Let your gift envelope dry completely. Here are some ideas of what you can give friends who come to your cultural celebration: a picture of yourself, a poem you wrote about the friend, something your friend collects, such as stickers or bottle caps, or anything else you'd like to give that fits into the envelope.

© 1999 Gary Braman

Gifts of the Wise Men

On January 6, many children in Spain receive gifts for *Epiphany* (pronounced ee-PIF-ih-nee). Children believe that the Three Wise Men who brought gifts to the baby Jesus will bring them gifts on this holiday. Children leave a pair of shoes out at night, hoping to find a special gift inside the shoes the next morning.

Read These Books to Learn More

Armando Araneda, José. *A Family in Bolivia.* Lerner, 1986.

Ayo, Yvonne. *Africa.* Eyewitness Books series. Knopf, 1995.

Baquedano, Elizabeth. *Aztec, Inca, and Maya.* Eyewitness Books series. Knopf, 1993.

Coil, Suzanne M. *Mardi Gras!* Macmillan, 1994.

Corbett, Sara. *Shake, Rattle, and Strum.* Children's Press, 1995.

Fox, Mary Virginia. *Papua, New Guinea.* Enchantment of the World series. Children's Press, 1994.

Haldane, Suzanne. *Painting Faces.* Dutton, 1988.

Hintz, Martin. *Ghana.* Enchantment of the World series. Children's Press, 1987.

Hoyt-Goldsmith, Diane. *Pueblo Storyteller.* Holiday House, 1991.

McLenighan, Valjean. *China: A History to 1949.* Enchantment of the World series. Children's Press, 1983.

McNair, Sylvia. *India.* Enchantment of the World series. Children's Press, 1990.

McNair, Sylvia. *Korea.* Enchantment of the World series. Children's Press, 1986.

Murdoch, David. *North American Indian.* Eyewitness Books series. Knopf, 1995.

Temko, Florence. *Traditional Crafts from Mexico and Central America.* Lerner, 1996.

Glossary

adinkra   The name of a dye; also means "good-bye."

Amish   A religious group who came to America in the 1700s from Germany and France.

bamboo   A tropical woody grass with hard stems.

eucalyptus   A tall tree native to Australia.

fetish   An object believed to have magical or spiritual powers.

fray   To wear away.

henna   A natural, reddish brown dye.

ideograph   A graphic symbol that is used to express an idea.

kente   (from the word *kenten* meaning "basket") A type of Ghanaian cloth woven in designs that look like basket weaving.

kilt   A knee-length plaid skirt with deep pleats.

mosque   A place where Muslims pray.

nephrite   A type of jade that is white to dark green in color.

nuns   Women who belong to a religious order.

page   A young man who delivers messages or does errands.

papyrus   A grasslike plant whose stems are used as a writing material.

powwow   A gathering of tribes where Indians can celebrate their culture.

reeds   Hollow stems of tall grasses.

sarcophagus   (plural **sarcophagi**) Stone coffin.

Shaker   Member of a Christian religious group who originally came from England and settled in North America in the 1700s; also the simple, functional, and well-crafted style in which a Shaker object is made.

shaman   A person who acts as a communication link between humans and spirits.

symmetry   Balance in which one side of a design is the mirror image of the other side.

totora   A hollow-stemmed grass that grows around Lake Titicaca, which lies between Peru and Bolivia in South America.

index

Guatemalan weaving, 12
Gyaman, 18

H

Haida Indians, 27
Halloween, 73
Hanukkah, 89
Hawaiian dancers, 86
headdress, 73, 82–85, 89
    Amazonian Indian, 82–83, 89
    Micronesian, 85
hei tiki, 49–51
    necklace, 89
    pendant, 49–50
henna, 87
Hindu, 95
homemade dough, 1, 2, 22, 36,
    54, 92
Honduras, 30
Horsley, John Callcott, 94
Huichol Indians, 75, 77
hula dance, 86

I

ideograph, 27
Imani, 97
Inca, 27–28
Incan quipu, 27

India, 6, 45, 87, 95
    Calcutta, 45
    southern, 6
Indians, American, 5–6, 24–25, 30, 42,
    55, 73
    Arawak, 99
    Carib, 99
    of Pacific Northwest, 77
    Quiché, 13
Indian ankle bracelet, 86–87
Indian welcome message, 5
Indonesia, 3, 20
Inuit, 27, 53, 78
Inuit animal sculpture, 53
Italian carnival mask, 78–79
    half-mask, 79
Italy, 43
    Venice, 21, 72, 79

J

Jalisco, 59
Japan, 102
    actors in, 73
    theater in, 81
Japanese mizuhiki, 101–102
Java, 20
Jesus, 104
Jewish people, 101